AFRICAN ICONS

AFRICAN ICONS

Ten People Who Shaped History

TRACEY BAPTISTE

illustrated by Hillary D. Wilson

ALGONQUIN YOUNG READERS   2021

Published by
Algonquin Young Readers
an imprint of Algonquin Books of Chapel Hill
Post Office Box 2225
Chapel Hill, North Carolina 27515-2225

a division of
Workman Publishing
225 Varick Street
New York, New York 10014

LIBRARY OF CONGRESS CATALOGING-IN-PUBLICATION DATA

Names: Baptiste, Tracey, author. | Wilson, Hillary D., illustrator.
Title: African icons : ten people who shaped history / Tracey Baptiste ;
illustrated by Hillary D. Wilson.
Description: First edition. | Chapel Hill : Algonquin Young Readers, 2021. |
Includes bibliographical references and index. | Audience: Ages 9–12 | Audience:
Grades 4–6 | Summary: "Full-color portraits illustrate the stories of ten people—
rulers, educators, inventors, scholars, and explorers—who helped shape the
African continent and the world from ancient times through the tumultuous
sixteenth century"—Provided by publisher.
Identifiers: LCCN 2021011317 | ISBN 9781616209001 (hardcover) |
ISBN 9781643752303 (ebook)
Subjects: LCSH: Africa—Biography—Juvenile literature. | Africa—Kings and rulers—
Biography—Juvenile literature. | Africa—History—Juvenile literature.
Classification: LCC DT18 .B37 2021 | DDC 960.099—dc23
LC record available at https://lccn.loc.gov/2021011317

10 9 8 7 6 5 4 3 2 1
First Edition

For Uncle Leo
(March 1927 to May 2020)

and for all African descendants
whose stories were taken away.

CONTENTS

INTRODUCTION: WHEN AFRICA FUELED THE WORLD

When I was little, my father told me a story about a hunter who found a skull in the bush. It went like this:

> *A man tripped over a human skull as he was hunting in the bush. "How did you get here?" the man asked. To his surprise, the skull answered, "Talking got me here." The hunter was shocked and ran to his village to tell everyone what he found. Naturally, everyone wanted to see this talking skull, including the king, so the hunter led them back. He asked the skull again, "How did you get here?" But the skull said nothing. The hunter asked again and again, but the skull was still silent. Eventually the king got angry and ordered the hunter's head cut off on the spot. As soon as everyone went home, the skull said, "And how did you get here?" The hunter's head replied, "Talking got me here."*

I didn't know that this story of the hunter and the skull is one of the most popular stories throughout the continent of Africa. The story my father told is closest to "The Talking Skull" by the Nupe people of Nigeria. My father is of Indian descent and was born and raised on the Caribbean island of Trinidad, which is simply proof of how stories made their way around and how connected Africa has always been to the rest of the world.

If I were to tell you a story about thieves who hid their loot in a mountain cave and who needed a password for the mountain to open up and let them into their lair, you might think of the Arabian story "Ali Baba and the Forty Thieves." There is an African story called "The Password" from the Dahomey people of West Africa that is very much the same. If I mention a story about a giant and a man who tricked it, you might think about the English story "Jack the Giant Killer," but there is a similar story called "A-Man-Among-Men" from the Hausa people of Nigeria.

African stories, like African culture, beliefs, technology, and people, have been moving around the world for centuries. I find it interesting, then, that in the United States, when people think of Black History, it is often limited to enslavement, the Civil War, and the civil rights movement. At the beginning of Black History Month every February 1, when my children would come home from school with a Black History project—often questions on a single sheet of paper—I would have to remind them that the people who were brought to the Americas and forced into bondage had rich lives prior to their theft and enslavement by Europeans. Imagine having the lengthy history of the first people on the planet, living on the second-largest continent on Earth, all whittled down to a single sheet of paper. That's some sheet.

I hope, in this book, to bring to life some of the history of Africa *before* the forcible transportation of so many via the Middle Passage to enslavement in Europe, the Americas, and the Caribbean. Through examining the lives of ten fascinating and unique Africans, I want to shed light on what was happening to the African land they lived on and how they helped to shape the lives of people on the continent and in the wider world. In so doing, I also hope to correct some inaccuracies about what was happening in Africa before enslavement and colonialism ravaged it.

The best place to start examining the early history of Africa is by looking at the land itself. We all have a distorted view of the African continent, thanks to disproportional maps. Africa is a lot bigger than you think. At 11,677,239 square miles, it takes up one-fifth of the total land area of Earth. The continent stretches for five thousand miles from Cape Verde in the north to the Cape of Good Hope on the southern tip. It is nearly as wide across. The only continent larger than Africa is Asia. The most commonly used map, the Mercator projection, shows Africa 14.5 times smaller than it actually is in proportion to other countries, while showing places like Europe, Russia, the United States, and Greenland much larger than they really are. Graphic artist Kai Krause created a map that compares the actual size of Africa to various countries.

Not only is Africa the second largest continent on Earth but the history of Africa is also the longest of anywhere on Earth. Early humans appeared in Africa over two million years ago and evolved into *Homo sapiens*, or modern humans, about two hundred thousand years ago. About seventy thousand years

THE TRUE SIZE OF AFRICA

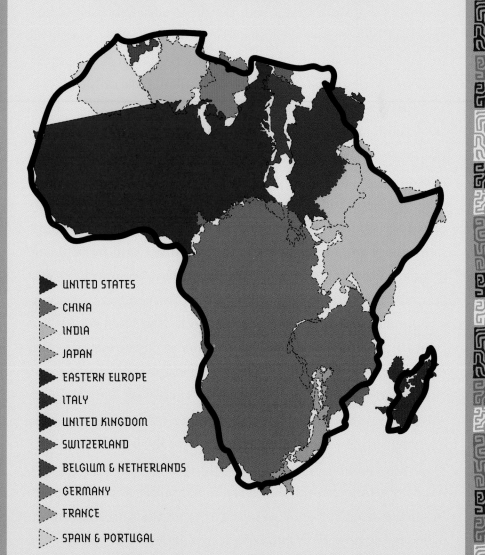

- UNITED STATES
- CHINA
- INDIA
- JAPAN
- EASTERN EUROPE
- ITALY
- UNITED KINGDOM
- SWITZERLAND
- BELGIUM & NETHERLANDS
- GERMANY
- FRANCE
- SPAIN & PORTUGAL

ago, Africans developed language; created art, tools, and hunting technology; and began moving out of the continent and populating the entire planet. The single language developed by Africans fifty thousand to seventy thousand years ago is the root of all six thousand languages spoken around the world today. This original African language was complex, and it used a combination of sounds, including clicks. The very first languages to evolve from it were developed in eastern Africa in what is now Tanzania, Kenya, and Ethiopia. The enduring "click" languages of some African countries have more than one hundred sounds, while some newer languages, like Hawaiian, have only thirteen. English uses forty-five sounds.

Today, there are between four hundred and one thousand African languages, each reflecting the unique culture of its people.

Six thousand years ago, as the landscape and climate changed, African people started moving across the continent, following better hunting opportunities and more fertile ground. Along the way, they developed new communities and complex forms of governments, some of which were matrilineal, some patrilineal. By 3000 BCE, gold had been discovered beneath African soil. Discovery of gold and other precious minerals changed agricultural communities into the world's very first kingdoms and empires. One of these was Kemit, which means "the black lands." It was so named by the people who lived there because of the rich mud of the Nile River. Later, foreigners began to call it Egypt. This kingdom formed in northeastern Africa, starting around 3100 BCE. To its south was the Kingdom of Kush, located in Nubia, as much of the land south of Egypt was called at the time. This kingdom consolidated its power starting around 1000 BCE. Three Kushite kingdoms ruled in Nubia for over three thousand years. The last was the Kingdom of Meroë, which was named for the capital city at the time of this reign. Though it's important to note that civilizations existed in north-eastern Africa long before Egypt and Kush consolidated into kingdoms, other kingdoms developed in sub-Saharan Africa when trade routes were etched across the vast desert. With its many natural resources, Africa drew international attention, and its people became traders both within the continent and across the Mediterranean and Red Seas, exporting African gold, art, and culture to the rest of the world.

African Icons: Ten People Who Shaped History is an introduction to the story of this great continent and its people. A trek across Africa to do in-person research was impossible, so I turned to libraries that focus on African history, like the African Studies Library at Boston University; to museums like the Metropolitan Museum of Art in New York City; and to online sources such as Academia.edu, where people who are doing academic research all over the world publish their findings. Librarians, art histo-rians, professors, and researchers were only too happy to help me. Every email I sent was returned with helpful information, and every meeting I had was met with a willingness to share as much as I could record. However, the search was frustrating at times. An interesting snippet in one source might be impossible to verify or expand on. Much of the older research about African history is riddled with the bias of people who viewed Africa and Africans as inferior to their own culture and lineage. Now that African scholars are telling the stories of their own continent, true African history is being revealed. I am excited to see the findings that are yet to come.

THE SAHARA YAWNS

For millennia, ancient Africans thrived on a continent of multiple landscapes. There were lush forests, ice-capped mountains, volcanic craters, grassy plains, serrated peaks, marshlands, treacherous rivers, deltas teeming with wild animals, and eventually, formed over thousands of years, the formidable desert: the Sahara. Without claws, horns, hooves, or tough hide, humans had to adapt quickly for their own protection and survival. They paid close attention to the land, the weather, the sky, and every creature around them, from the enormous, vicious aurochs, a now-extinct species of wild cattle, to the tiniest tsetse fly, whose bite could cause sleeping sickness and fever. They honed their hunting skills and developed ever better tools and weapons. The first bows and arrows appeared around 62,000 BCE. Following on the heels of this new hunting technology came spring traps. These used the same principles of tension and release as bows and arrows and could be set and left as hunters did other work. Knives advanced from whittled stone to blades that could be attached to wooden handles and were made of forged iron with razor-sharp edges on one side and blunt, curved edges on the other. In the earliest example of applied chemistry, Africans developed glue to assemble these tools. They learned to heat it to a precise temperature that allowed them to attach the blade to the handle without weakening either the blade or the handle. This made it possible to have tools and weapons that could be used multiple times, rather than single-use projectiles like wooden arrows.

As their understanding of chemical compounds evolved, Africans developed a new hunting weapon: poison. These poisons were cleverly composed to fell huge ancient beasts but have no ill effects on the people who would eat the meat after.

Africans used the available raw materials they had to their advantage, and they used them with flair. When hunters set out, they left behind shelters made of natural materials outfitted with soft cloth bedding stuffed with insect-repelling plants. Their walls were covered in artistic carvings and pigmented paintings. When they pursued game, bows and arrows in hand, they took along ever sturdier spears and knives covered with geometric carvings that reflected each hunter's ownership and sense of pride. Water canteens made of ostrich eggshells were delicately carved, with water spouts attached for easy drinking. Beautifully whittled whistles were used to send melodic messages to fellow hunters over long distances.

About 6,000 years ago, the land was beginning to change beneath Africans' feet. The earth's tilt, which is always shifting slightly, had made enough of a move that a large portion of land in north Africa that was once thick with trees and plants began to dry out. Over the course of 5,000 years, the land went from green and moist to dry and sandy. Those in the northeast of the continent, who had developed the Arabic language, recognized this new landscape at once as a "sahra," or desert, which gave the desert its name: Sahara. The dry, sandy landscape eventually would stretch to 3.3 million square miles, roughly the size of the United States, making it the largest hot desert in the world. The vast, waterless, intensely hot Sahara squeezed communities in northern Africa toward the coasts.

The countries south of the desert, in what is called sub-Saharan Africa, would have a different history than the countries to the north, who were connected by land or a short water voyage to Europe and the Middle East. In the northern part of the continent, agricultural societies formed where the ground was wet and rich enough for planting. The first major African communities came together around a length of fertile ground to the east, along the banks of the Nile River. One was Kush; the other, Egypt.

With the Nile flowing through their land, the scorching Sahara to their west, and rough seas to the east, the Kushites and the Egyptians enjoyed abundant lives free from outside influence. Within their borders, however, there was turmoil.

MENES: CREATOR OF DYNASTIES

{Mee-neez}

In the thirty-first century BCE, Egypt was a country of many minor kings, and the land was split in two. Upper Egypt was a country of cities where people clustered close to land viable for fishing and hunting. Lower Egypt had more farmland, fed by the waters of the Nile River, with fewer cities than its neighbor. The lands were named according to the flow of the Nile, and because the river flowed from south to north, Upper Egypt lay to the south, while Lower Egypt was north, close to the Mediterranean Sea. Both groups shared the same language, customs, and religious beliefs.

The Nile, flowing upward through the country, split and bent and split again into six main sections called cataracts, which were bursting with life. Hulking hippopotamuses and snapping crocodiles lurked alongside silver pike that could grow up to six feet long and red-tailed catfish that swam beneath the river's surface. Papyrus reeds waved on the banks of the river, covering the shore in lush green and providing cover for vicious animals that lay in wait for prey.

Despite the dangers, the Nile was busy. People bathed in open shores where they could see a threat coming, and boats traveled up and down the waters. Some boats were for the pleasure of the families of kings; others were used for trade and transport.

The Nile was life and death, pleasure and commerce, beauty and pain. Every year, the river rose and overflowed, spilling into the banks, saturating the land and making it soft and fertile, perfect for farming. Northern farmers, ankle-deep in rich mud, had no problems coaxing cotton, wheat, beans, corn, figs, and other crops from the Nile's shores. There was plenty to feed their own families and extra to trade north over the Mediterranean and south to Upper Egypt. The bounty of the river meant that not everyone needed to farm in order to eat. People branched out into other occupations. Craftworkers made tools for farmers, chisels for artists working in stone and copper, and even needles for sewing. Potters used the mud from the Nile to make pots and jars for storing food and other items. They also made cooking utensils and religious vessels that would store organs during mummification. Some pottery was made purely for decorative use. Beneath the ground lay minerals that kept Egyptians wealthy and gave them the means to trade with other countries: turquoise, carnelian, granite, and electrum were all available for those who dug deep enough.

It was during this time of thriving agriculture and trade that a young king named Menes, who ruled over cities in Upper Egypt, including Thinis, Heirakonpolis, and Naqada, looked to expand his territory. Menes was just twenty-five years old. His people enjoyed trade with other regions, not only in Egypt, but stretching south into Kush. But the cities Menes ruled over didn't have direct access to the farmlands of Lower Egypt. Controlling the farmland would give him the ability to feed his people easily, and his already tight control over southern urban centers would secure continued wealth from trade.

Menes's takeover of Upper and Lower Egypt was built on a series of military expeditions. Beginning just before 3032 BCE, Menes began conquering the lands surrounding his kingdom. In campaign after campaign he took the fight to neighboring kings, capturing their territories with brutal force. He was no reluctant leader. He rode in with his army, brandishing the tools of war, taking enemies by the neck, and crushing them with his own hands. While no historical account explains what made

Menes such an exceptional and virtually unbeatable foe, we do know that he was called the Scorpion King, perhaps because he was quick and formidable and struck with deadly force.

With most of Upper Egypt under his banner, Menes set his sights north, on Lower Egypt and its rich farmland. Menes extracted the loyalty of lesser kings by agreement, at the point of a weapon, or simply by killing them off. But even conquered, the Egyptians from different areas were frustratingly fractured. Menes had forced them to answer to him, but he couldn't yet force them to get along with one other. Menes had to find a way to deal with this infighting to have any hope of holding on to the power he had squeezed from his enemies. His armies had already killed anyone loyal to the leaders he conquered, people who might attempt revenge or try to take his new power. But Menes had to unite his new subjects and ensure their loyalty in order for his hold over Egypt to be secure. How could he get the hard-won and bloody unification of Upper and Lower Egypt to last?

The answer was religion.

The falcon god Horus was one of Egypt's most significant deities. Horus ruled the land of Egypt. His right eye, the sun and morning star, stood for power. His left eye, the moon and evening star, stood for healing. Religious groups that worshipped Horus existed throughout the land. It was a commonality among the warring factions that Menes could exploit.

Menes declared that Horus himself had bestowed the kingship of Egypt on him, and that furthermore Menes was not simply a follower of the god, but was a god in his own right, a living embodiment of Horus on Earth.

Who would dare oppose a living god who had a brutally efficient army?

Menes' clever move also ensured that his lineage would continue to rule after he was gone, because divinity, of course, was inherited. It would pass from father to son. With this declaration, Menes began the first dynasty of a united Egypt—and began a tradition that would have a long-lasting effect on the history, politics, and religion of the country. Bestowing on himself the divine right to rule meant that every ruler after him could assume the same level of power, the same indisputable right over any and all, and could be assured the one kind of loyalty that was more powerful than blood relation. Menes is considered Egypt's first pharaoh, a term that means "great house." Menes himself would not have been called this in his lifetime, however, because the term "pharaoh" was not used to refer to the king until the eighteenth dynasty in 1539 BCE.

Menes' metamorphosis into a god was further boosted by another decision, this one a clever costume change.

The kings of Upper Egypt traditionally wore a white woven war crown, called a "hedjet," which was peaked in the middle. The kings of Lower Egypt wore a red crown, called a "deshret," that was bowl-shaped, had a peak at the back, and had a curled piece that jutted out from the front center. Menes combined the white hedjet crown of Upper Egypt with the red deshret crown of Lower Egypt. Together, the double crown became a new symbol of power for the pharaoh. The symbolism of the two crowns together was so powerful as a physical representation of the new order of things that the double crown would remain a symbol of the pharaoh for several dynasties, spanning hundreds of years.

With this costume change, Menes was also playing on a prevailing cultural and religious belief: the Egyptian idea of duality, the idea that two separate things could exist in one. In Egyptian mythology, the god Set, for example, was seen as unhappy, violent, and connected with chaos and the desert. The god Osiris, Set's exact opposite, was connected to happiness, calm, orderliness, and life and was to be found in the waters of the river Nile. Together, they represented a duality of good and evil. Set, as a trickster, also had a dual personality, since tricks could be beneficial or destructive.

After Menes brought Upper and Lower Egypt together, the country as a whole was referred to as the Two Lands. But Menes wasn't done cementing his place as ruler and deity. He married Benerib, a princess from one of the families he conquered when he rode into Lower Egypt. The match meant that the royal family was now a combination of both Upper and Lower Egypt, and the moment Menes and Benerib had a child, that child would belong to all of Egypt, not a country split across the middle.

With his rule over the Two Lands firmly established, Menes needed to find a suitable place from which to rule. When he took the kingship, the capital of Upper Egypt, Abydos, lay far to the south, nowhere close to Lower Egypt. Menes needed to rule from somewhere more central to all his people. He decided to move the capital to a location at the border between the two regions. The move would further cement the two regions as one. But building the capital was no easy feat. One of the cataracts of the Nile ran right through what Menes thought was the ideal location, which made it waterlogged. To build the new capital there, Menes would have to literally move part of the Nile.

The work of drying up part of the river was mathematically precise, meticulously managed, and backbreakingly difficult. Under a hot Egyptian sun, hundreds of men, mostly farmers who were working in the months after the harvest was done, labored to realize Menes' vision. They brought wood up from beyond the southern borders and the country of the neighboring kingdom, Kush. This was used to construct dams and reroute the river.

Once the dams were in place and the river diverted, an island was created right in the center. Menes had the capital built on this island. The architecture of the new capital was incredible. Fortified buildings of solid brick with three chambers stood overlooking the desert like sentinels. These whitewashed buildings would become a staple of Egyptian architecture and would later evolve into the many-chambered pyramids we all know well. It earned the city the name White Walls. Later, it would be renamed Memphis. The people of Egypt, in their modest homes of mud brick, built to withstand the heat, and the nomadic people who traveled the dunes and spent their nights in tents on the sands of the Sahara must have been struck with awe by the sight of the formidable buildings lined up in a row and reflecting the sunlight off their pristine walls like gold.

One of the three original buildings at Memphis was set aside as Menes' palace. It was constructed as a rectangle on top of a rectangle, reaching upward like stairs into the sky, the realm of the god Horus. False doors of recessed rectangles decorated the outside walls and were painted brightly in red, yellow, black, blue, and green, all pigments available from plants and minerals in the land. This rectangle-on-top-of-rectangle design became the symbol of kingship. It was used on seals that would be stamped on doors and as decorations designed for members of the royal family and the high priests who served them. Just as Menes himself was the living embodiment of Horus on Earth, the palace was the architectural representative of him to the people who weren't afforded the opportunity to see him behind those gleaming white palace walls.

Once completed, Memphis would become the center of the Egyptian economy. The most important marketplaces, palaces, and temples were all built there. And its importance endured for millennia. Modern-day Cairo, today the capital of Egypt, is located where Memphis was.

With Egypt conquered and the capital established, Menes remained within his palace doing the administrative work of running the country. The people he had conquered would rarely see him out and about. They did, however, see the governors Menes appointed to rule over the cities and smaller districts that made up Egypt. Governors would go out into these areas, and each would report back to the palace. One man, a vizier, which translates to "supervisor of everything in this entire land," received all the reports, and he would take them to the pharaoh.

Egypt settled under Menes' rule, and his time as pharaoh was peaceful. There was plenty of food, security at Egypt's borders and within the country, and a hierarchical political system that was working well. Wealth abounded, allowing for the further development of religion, art, recreation, and sport. In the farmers' off seasons, they were contracted to work as builders, to accommodate the city's growth with new buildings and new water canals. The Egyptians paid their builders in beer, which they brewed from the abundant wheat.

Menes' literal and mythological control of Egypt was a roaring success. He united Upper and Lower Egypt, brought peace to the land, established a working government, and got the people to accept him as a god on Earth. So it is perhaps no surprise that Menes' death also took on mythological significance.

At the age of sixty-two, after thirty-two years of rule, Menes was out on the Nile when he was attacked and killed by a hippopotamus. For the Egyptians, the symbolism of this death further cemented the idea of Menes as the god Horus. Horus had a rival, his uncle Set, who was depicted as a hippopotamus. In Egyptian mythology, Set was the lord of the scorching sands of the desert, and he represented chaos. Hieroglyphs recount the brutal battles in which Set tried again and again to kill Horus and to overthrow him but was never successful. But with the manner of Menes' death, the mythology must have seemed to have taken a frighteningly realistic turn.

The sudden loss of the pharaoh in such a violent manner would have led to a tumultuous time even without the obvious symbolism. It is likely that Menes' wives and their sons immediately began infighting as each son vied for the right to be heir to the throne. Menes had built his power by spilling the blood of his enemies, and his eventual heir would have to do the same. Only this time the killings would come from inside the palace walls, culled from his own circle of friends and family, and not from the kings he had conquered to become the first ruler of the first dynasty.

Power in Egypt, it seemed, always came with brutal force. It is not known how many wives Menes had, but three were chief among them: Benerib, the princess from Lower Egypt Menes had married, along with Khenthap and Neithotep. The next king would be one of their sons. But until the family drama was sorted out, someone needed to be in charge of the day-to-day administration of Egypt. Neithotep stepped into this role. As queen, she took on the role of regent until the new pharaoh was decided on. She probably assumed the role believing that it would be one of her own sons who would take Menes' place on the throne, but that was not to be. Eventually, Djer, the son of Khenthap, was chosen as the next pharaoh. How he came to be the victor is unknown.

While the family was settling the question of succession, Menes' body was being prepared for burial. Mummification typically took about seventy days. As the second pharaoh of Egypt, it was Djer's right and duty to send his father off to the afterlife with all the honor and ceremony afforded to a god. That meant gold, jewels, food, and beer.

It also meant death for the family members and servants who would accompany Menes in the afterlife. Djer would have overseen the deaths of hundreds. He chose carefully, culling those brothers who would have been a threat to his rule, their mothers who would have sought revenge, and any servants and nobles who favored his rivals over him. It was a gruesome task. But whatever love he felt for those walking into death didn't matter. All that mattered was the orderly, albeit bloody, transfer of power. He had been raised to understand that and to do what he must to ensure that the transition of power to him went unchallenged. The weapons used would have been spears and knives, so the bloodletting would have been lengthy, as well as loud from the pain of the victims, the fear of those waiting, and the mourning of those who were left behind.

The mummified remains of Menes and those who died to join him in the afterlife were placed in boats and sailed up the Nile river to Abydos, the old capital, which had become the new center of religion and would be the resting place for all leaders and their families. Djer, the new pharaoh, took his place at the back of the lead boat. The fleet fought the Nile's currents on their eight- or nine-day journey south to where Menes would be buried, in an aboveground burial site called a "mastaba," a massive rectangular tomb made of mud brick to house the bodies of dead royals. The mastaba's walls sloped gently to a flat roof that sheltered the many comforts that would follow the deceased into the afterlife: food, drink, riches. A deep shaft beneath the tomb led to the burial chamber, where the mummified remains of the dead were interred. Wider than they were tall, built to withstand the elements, mastabas were mainly utilitarian and not meant to be pretty.

On board also were living servants, family members, and nobles packed up for the days-long journey there and back—though not all of them would return. Servants and some nobles who had not yet crossed over into the afterlife were slated to die when they arrived at Abydos. Their blood would be spilled at the foot of Menes's tomb, and they all knew it when they stepped on board.

Menes' boldness in becoming Egypt's first pharaoh launched a historic series of dynasties that would last for over 3,000 years, ending with the death of the last pharaoh, Cleopatra. The Egyptian dynasties remain by far the longest rule of any empire or dynasty in the world. The divine right of the pharaohs was the first and most stable government of its kind in world history. And it all began with a young, ambitious military leader named Menes. It would be an impressive accomplishment for anyone, but was especially so for Menes, who united Egypt when he was only thirty years old and ruled for more than thirty years.

MERNEITH: A QUEEN ERASED

{Murr-**neeth**}

Some of the enduring figures of African history are important not for the record of what they did, but for what they left behind and for what those remainders tell us about the time and place in which they lived. Such is the case with Queen Merneith, Menes' granddaughter and Djer's daughter, whose life was barely recorded, but whose tomb reflected her status as regent and queen mother and was filled with treasures that have helped unlock mysteries about her.

The Memphis in which Merneith grew up was a wonder. The city Pharaoh Menes had dredged from the Nile River had never been seen before. The palace Menes built, which was inherited by his son and heir, Pharaoh Djer, was stunning. High white walls around the palace kept the desert heat at bay, while the royal family lived inside a large network of rooms and courtyards whose doors were inset with multihued decorations, some created to look like native Egyptian plants.

Only those who lived inside the palace walls knew of its beauty and comfort, a comfort afforded to few outside. All the wives and royal children would have had several servants to cater to their needs. There were servants to bathe and oil them—several times a day—with wood- and flower-scented fragrances to combat the oppressive Egyptian heat. There were servants to cook the food, to serve the food, and to clean up after the meals. The wives were outfitted in the finest linens woven from the flax of Egypt's shores, while tapestries from abroad lined the rooms or were sewn into cushions for the royal family to lounge on. The rooms were scented with Lebanese cedarwood, and imported wines flowed in cups, alongside beer from Egypt's own wheat. Ornate jewelry made of gold mined from African soil just south or west of Egypt, as well as bright red carnelian and turquoise from Sinai, an Egyptian peninsula that jutted into the Middle East, dripped from royal necks and wrists. Scented wax cones placed on the nobles' heads melted perfume down their bodies in the Egyptian heat. In this luxurious atmosphere, a young girl named Merneith was born and raised to rule.

A royal physician was available at any time, day or night, checking on everything from the wives' teeth to the births of new royal children. The children had nursemaids to care for them and instructors to teach them, and the nursery and walled-in courtyards were noisy with their outdoor games: wrestling, dancing, and sports that resembled modern-day javelin throwing, tug-of-war, and handball. Inside, the children played quieter games, like senet, a game with small pieces and a board, similar to checkers. If the pharaoh, the vizier, the governors, and the priests wanted to work, they could move to closed-door chambers in the palace far away from the children.

It was a decadent life for the young Merneith. But she would not have seen only luxury. Living close to her grandfather, Menes, and her father, Djer, she would also have observed the many comings and goings of the country's administrators, advisers, and priests, and she would have understood the work of running Egypt. That turned out to be a good thing.

Like the death of Pharaoh Menes before him, the death of Merneith's father, Pharaoh Djer, caused tumult. The royal sons, once calmly—if not entirely pleasantly—coexisting, immediately began to jockey to see who would be the next king. With that jockeying came alliances and allegiances broken and made. Blood turned against blood, because it was by blood that the next king would be named. Merneith saw it all firsthand. After ruling for nearly six decades, her father, Djer, was gone, and she had little time to mourn as the rest of the royal household scrambled to decide on the new king and align themselves with whoever they thought would come out on top.

Merneith's brother, Djet, was the eventual front-runner in the family haggling, but the drama was far from over. Now Djet would decide the exact tribute his father would get with his burial. Djet oversaw the killing of nearly six hundred people to join Pharaoh Djer in the afterlife. Merneith walked on the edges of that horror until she was sure that she was not also slated for death. Though women were also killed to join the pharaoh, Merneith was perhaps too unimportant politically to be a threat, and being the daughter of the former king and the sister of the next one had its advantages. Many other women were not likely so lucky. The women near Egyptian kings were seen as important accessories to power, there for the purpose of giving birth to and raising the next generation of kings. Once that duty was fulfilled, they might have been expected to accompany the king to the afterlife as well.

Following Djer's funeral, Merneith became one of Djet's wives. Egyptians liked to keep power firmly within the family. Maintaining that continuity of power meant that it was not unusual for brothers and sisters of Egyptian royal families to be married, a practice that continued through Cleopatra's reign.

Djet's reign did not last long. Unlike his father and grandfather, he died a young man, leaving only boys as his heirs. None of them was old enough to rule, and the one chosen to succeed him, Merneith's son, Den, was barely ten years old. Without a pharaoh, the country would be thrown into chaos as the nobles in the royal palace vied for power and outside threats tried to take advantage of the lack of leadership. It was crucial to maintain order and keep the kingship in the family, but how?

As it so happened, there was a precedent for just this situation. When Menes died and the struggle over who would be the next pharaoh raged, one of his royal wives, Neithotep, had taken over as regent. It was a temporary queenly title which meant she would make decisions until the new pharaoh was decided on and could rule on his own. Like Neithotep, Merneith, wife and sister to Pharaoh Djet, took on the power as regent. Merneith stepped into the role knowing it would bring eventual rewards. In death, Neithhotep had been treated as a pharaoh, with a large burial tomb, the usual luxurious offerings for the dead, and an entourage to accompany her in the afterlife. Merneith would have known this and expected it for herself.

A brutal transition of power took place once again, this time with Merneith in charge. She oversaw the sacrificial killings of servants and family members who would go with Djet to the afterlife. But under Merneith, the tradition underwent significant changes, ones that made the transition somewhat less brutal. Unlike the two previous transitions, where many hundreds were killed, a mere 328 were chosen to make the ultimate sacrifice to accompany Djet. And while a stunning 85 percent of the sacrifices for her father, Djer, had been women, Merneith instead chose mostly men of the highest rank in society to accompany Djet. These men were most likely considered to be the greatest threats to her young son's throne and his throat.

After Djet's burial, Den, the child pharaoh, was taught how to rule his kingdom while his mother took the reins of the country. As regent, Queen Merneith was responsible for all the things a pharaoh would have been, including waging war, building monuments, and settling disputes. She ruled well, and the transfer of power to her son when he was of age went smoothly. But her legacy was not to last. Long after Den was gone, as the First Dynasty wound toward its end, Merneith's name was erased from the lists of rulers, the way women throughout history would often be erased from the record of those who made important contributions. The Egyptians soon forgot the queen who made sure that the transfer of power from her husband to her son was peaceful. And when, a thousand years later, a new set of pharaohs tried to associate themselves with the first pharaohs in order to legitimize their rule, Merneith was not mentioned. In addition, as a woman, and not *exactly* the monarch but a placeholder for the eventual king, her accomplishments were never heralded, or even recorded, as a king's would have been. In fact, the record of Den's duties includes items such as "The First Time for Counting Gold" in year four of his reign and a cattle census in year five, when it was actually Merneith who was still in charge.

It was only in death that Merneith's importance was recorded. When the queen died, Den did as was expected, sending her off with great fanfare, as had been done with Queen Regent Neithotep before her. Merneith, like her father and grandfather, was ferried up the Nile River to be buried at Abydos in the same location where all the pharaohs of the first and second dynasties were buried. Sunken into the Egyptian sand, her burial chamber was lined with mud bricks, plastered, and whitewashed like those of the pharaohs. Forty-one of the dead who accompanied her to the afterlife were fitted into small canals dug into the sand around the queen regent, each separated by a single brick wall so they would each have their own burial room.

In trenches outside were the rest of the dead, seventy-nine of them, buried like sentinels around the structure, their blood mixed with the desert sand. But inside, where Merneith herself was laid, the scene was more luxurious. Surrounding her body were pottery vessels filled with a feast to sustain her in the afterlife: beer, wine, and honey, among other foods.

Merneith's tomb as a whole was as grand as a pharaoh's. Like the rulers who went before her, she probably oversaw its construction—at least until Den was old enough to take over. She also had a second tomb at Saqqara that contained a few dozen dead. Her service to the pharaoh had earned Merneith the honor of a grand burial and indicated she was a person of high royal stature and power. Later archaeologists would find her name inscribed on the funerary stela near her tomb—a stone that typically stood upright in or near the tomb and had carved on it the name of and images or inscriptions about the deceased. A king list in another tomb also recorded her importance: Merneith's name was written between Pharaohs Djet and Den, with the label "King's Mother."

Were it not for the discovery of her tomb, along with the title "King's Mother" on seals on her tomb and that of her son, Den, and in king lists that traced the lineage of Egyptian monarchs, this briefly powerful queen would be entirely lost to history.

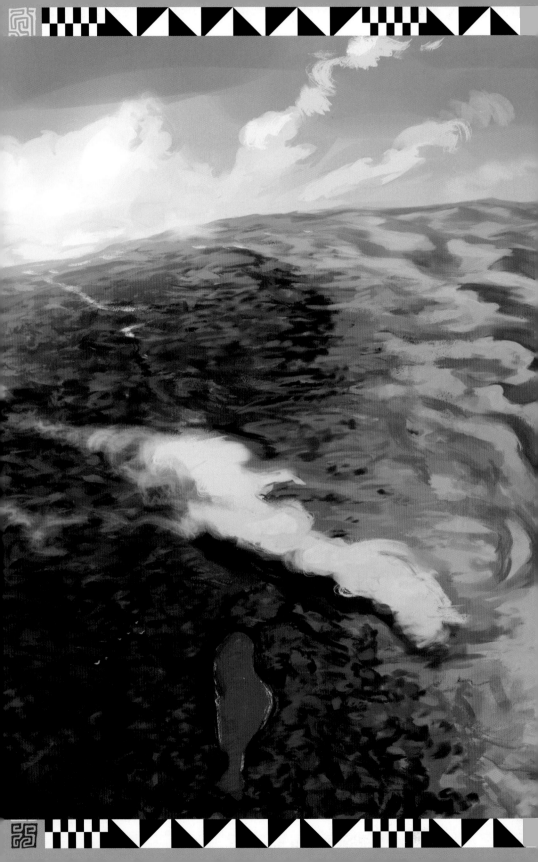

THE DAWN OF EGYPT

Rule in Egypt was measured by dynasties. Each dynasty was identified with the single common ancestor who began it. When there was no blood connection to the original ancestor, a new dynasty began. Trade flourished across the waters of the Mediterranean on the eastern shore, which made the country accessible to people across the sea. As trade flourished, influences from outside cultures seeped in.

Twenty-seventh-century BCE Egypt was at a crossroads of trade and culture. Land travel routes threaded through the country. Along these routes, merchants led camels laden with goods. From the south and the Kingdom of Kush, they brought gold and electrum. Granite, turquoise, carnelian, and other minerals came from mines within the country. Linen from Lower Egypt's shores was carried in bolts to be sold at markets both within Egypt's borders and in foreign bazaars. The banks of the Nile were crowded with papyrus reeds that provided the raw materials for paper, baskets, blankets, sandals, and even boats and medicine. Most of the papyrus was processed into paper across the Meditarranean, at Byblos, Lebanon, which is where the Bible got its name. Egypt's abundance of grain made its way to Rome.

At noisy seaports, the camels were off-loaded and goods were taken to boats by cart and by hand, carrying the best of what this small corner of Africa had to offer. From there, people and their wares went to places like Syria, Cyprus, Crete, and Greece. In exchange, Egypt got cedar from Lebanon, silks from Asia, cloth from the Middle East, olives from Italy, and many other goods from foreign countries. Popular trading ports were busy but treacherous. Thieves lay in wait to snatch goods, and local governments could do nothing unless the theft was by one of their own citizens. Without a means for justice, some victims would simply steal from others to make up their losses.

The markets and bazaars inside Egypt's borders also thrummed with activity. People could buy food like pork, grain, and bread; cloth and clothing; and makeup, art, baskets, pots, and jewelry (often made of copper because gold was so plentiful that the Egyptians traded it away). Also for sale were cedar and ebony wood, iron, ivory, and rare stones like lapis lazuli. Everywhere, the deben, a small, measured weight of copper, was being handed over for one type of object or another. The deben would help you quench your thirst quicker than it helped you get dressed. One deben earned you a liter of wine; two would buy you a pair of sandals; five, a shirt. Maybe that explains why so many of the people in Egyptian hieroglyphs are shirtless.

A bustling commercial center like this would seem to be the ideal place for someone to find fortune and rise to greatness. But Egypt was a place of strict hierarchy. The pharaoh ruled all, advised by the vizier. Next came the noble class, often the sons of pharaohs who were not destined to be pharaoh themselves. They maintained a strict administrative hold on the city and worked for the king by collecting taxes. High priests came next, then scribes, craftspeople, and merchants. But the majority of Egyptians were farmers working land along the Nile, with donkeys as their beasts of burden. When there was no farmwork because of the annual flooding of the Nile, these same farmers were recruited to construct the buildings that made up any one of the well-planned cities of Egypt.

With such a rigid social structure in place, it would be nearly impossible for anyone to rise above the station they were born to, but one young man named Imhotep seemed destined to do the impossible.

IMHOTEP: FROM PEASANT TO GOD

{Ihm-hoh-tep}

Born on the sixteenth day of Epiphi, third month of the harvest (what we now know as May 31) in the twenty-seventh century BCE in Ankhtowe, a town just outside of Memphis, the capital, Imhotep came into the world a mere mortal like the rest of us. Unlike the rest of us, he would not leave that way.

Son of an architect named Kanofer and a woman from the province of Mendes named Khreduonkh, Imhotep came from a family of no rank. He likely would have expected to become a builder and architect like his father.

Inside the palace walls at Memphis, the atmosphere near the end of the Second Dynasty, when Imhotep was a young boy, was fraught with political intrigue. The last pharaoh of the dynasty, Khasekhemwy, was ineffective. Outside those walls, direct evidence of his failed leadership was everywhere. Civil war plagued Egypt. The Upper and Lower lands were in turmoil, and infighting abounded. With so much strife within Egypt's borders, hostile neighbors from the north and south had spotted an advantage and were beginning to encroach on Egypt's land.

The Second Dynasty pharaohs had done away with the bloody sacrifices that marked the end of one pharaoh's reign and the beginning of the next. After Menes' dynasty ended, people were no longer killed to join the pharaoh in his afterlife. But the rulers of this new dynasty seemed incapable of keeping the peace. It's possible that political strife was set off by a famine that gripped Egypt and that the lack of food resources brought old rivalries to the surface. It's also possible that one of the Second Dynasty rulers decided to separate the Upper and Lower lands to stem the effects of the famine, pitting citizen against citizen.

What is clear is that all the accomplishments of the First Dynasty—centralized government, the beginning of an architectural style, a political system merged with religion, and the relative prosperity and safety of the country—were not enough to keep the hard-won peace that Menes had established more than five hundred years earlier.

By the time the last pharaoh of the Second Dynasty, Khasekhemwy, was in power, the country was unstable. Within the palace walls, the usual jockeying for power had reached a fever pitch. There to witness it all was the royal physician: Imhotep.

How or when Imhotep defied tradition and became doctor to the pharaoh and his family is unknown, but it did put him in a key position as the Second Dynasty drew to a close. Imhotep was caring for the dying pharaoh, and likely would have been with him in his last moments. It would have been his job to inform the royal family and advisers of the pharaoh's death. Then he could only stand back and watch as the thirst for power intoxicated those with something to gain in the rise of the next leader.

The young prince Djoser was pushed to the forefront by his mother, Nimaethap, but the title didn't go to him just yet. Nimaethap was the wife of Khasekhemwy, but Djoser was not his son by blood. First, Djoser's brother Nebka took the title and the throne.

Nebka's reign seems to have been quite brief. History is unclear on how or why, but we know Nebka's reign was not long enough for the king to have built his final resting place, as all previous kings had. The Unfinished Northern Pyramid of Zawyet El Aryan is ascribed by some to Nebka. However or whenever Nebka's reign ended, it was good news for Djoser, who now emerged as the next ruler.

Pharaoh Djoser was in a precarious position. He rose to

power after the tumultuous loss of two rulers in close succession, and as we know, the death of a ruler almost always led to strife and chaos. In addition, Djoser needed to secure Egypt's borders from encroachment by outside rulers and settle the internal hostility between the Upper and Lower lands. Even though Djoser would have been raised for kingship, watching as his father worked, he also relied on learned and capable people to advise him. Imhotep was not only one of those people but also became the king's most important adviser, given the title of vizier. Suddenly, a boy born of no rank was second only to the ruler of Egypt, effectively running the entire country when the new pharaoh was busy with other things.

The job of vizier involved giving political and religious advice, acting as the chief judge in the higher courts, and receiving daily reports from the governors and other ministers, such as those of the treasury, military, agriculture, and interior. These ministry positions were all held by nobles, most likely the siblings and cousins of Djoser—people who would have been born of higher rank than Imhotep but now answered to him.

Every morning, Imhotep got a report from each of the heads of different ministries responsible for the running of the country. If there was a judicial conflict that could not be resolved by judges of the lower court, Imhotep would step in and make the final decision.

With Imhotep taking care of the daily work of running the country, Djoser was free to quell the tensions between Upper and Lower Egypt and to take the military to the country's borders to secure them from outside invaders. Under Djoser, with Imhotep as vizier, order gradually returned to Egypt. Soon Djoser turned his attention to expanding Egypt's reach into Sinai, Libya, and south into Nubian land, all places they traded with, and which, if conquered, would enrich Egypt.

But just over a decade into Djoser's rule, another drought fell over Egypt. It continued for seven years. People were starving. Djoser was accused of bringing this tragedy on his people through his failure to honor the gods. Egyptians believed that the god Khnum, who ruled the Nile, was angry. One night, Djoser dreamed that the god had come to him to complain. Khnum told the pharaoh that his temple was in ruins, and the god was angry that people no longer worshipped him as they should have. In the morning, the pharaoh consulted with Imhotep and a governor named Medir. They concluded that the pharaoh should sail the Nile to the island Elephantine, where the temple to the god Khnum was built, and investigate for himself. If the temple needed repair or replacement, he should fix it right away. Upon arrival, Djoser saw that the temple was, in fact, in ruins, just as the god had told him. With his dream confirmed, Djoser had a new temple built on the foundation of the old one, and miraculously, the waters of the Nile rose again and the drought ended.

The people of Egypt were so pleased with Djoser's actions to save them that his deeds became legend. Djoser's rebuilding of the temple to satisfy the god and refill the waters of the Nile would become a story that was passed down for hundreds of years and was eventually written down on the Famine Stela, an inscription from the final Egyptian dynasty, the Ptolemaic, of the famed Cleopatra.

With Egypt's borders secure, and riding high from miraculously ending a famine, Djoser turned to improving the country's architecture. Before becoming a doctor, Imhotep had been trained as an architect by his father. Now Djoser ordered

Imhotep to oversee the building of new cities. Imhotep used his considerable talents to erect buildings more complex and ornate than past kings had done. But Djoser wanted to create something even more grand. Like the kings before him, he began to think of his legacy. What would he leave behind for his people to remember him, and where would he spend the afterlife?

Until then, royals had been buried in mastabas. While some mastabas were impressive, built up to twenty feet high, Djoser had something even grander in mind. Once again, he turned to Imhotep.

What Imhotep conceived of had never been made anywhere in the world. Instead of a single mastaba—or even a double one, with one tomb on top of the other, as had been made for some previous kings—Imhotep wanted to build six mastabas, each set on top of the other, getting smaller in size as they went, as if they were steps leading upward into the heavens. It was the world's first pyramid, the first large-scale building construction, the first building to be constructed out of solid stone instead of the traditional mud brick, and the first recorded instance of an architect's name that was written down for credit.

The Step Pyramid was built at Saqqara. It took twenty years to complete, is nearly two hundred feet at its base and is equally tall, and contains many inner chambers. Because the burial chambers were filled with treasures to accompany the pharaoh in the afterlife, the threat of grave robbers was high. Imhotep took extraordinary steps to keep thieves at bay. He had a series of mazes built beneath the pyramid. Outside, there were fourteen doors, but only one of them was real. The other thirteen false doors were carved imitations, complete with locks, but made out of solid stone—impossible to open. Several dummy chambers were built into the complex and filled with sand and gravel. Any thief trying to get in would be instantly buried in rubble and would suffocate to death. The king's treasure was lowered through a narrow vertical shaft one hundred feet belowground into a corridor; both shaft and corridor would have been dug out by hand. This kind of excavation would have been monumental and laborious without the use of machines. Farmers between planting and harvesting time would have had to use small vessels to scoop out the dirt, a job that likely took weeks.

Imhotep also brought great artistic sensibility to the project. All the buildings of the complex—the temple for Djoser's use, as well as two buildings behind it that the pharaoh was to use for hosting dignitaries—were designed for beauty. The complex was surrounded by forty sculpted posts that held up the ceiling. It featured carved trees, reeds, and other plant life that were then covered with bright green ceramic to make the plants look realistic. The walls of Djoser's burial chamber were covered in blue tile.

The sheer size and labor force involved in building the Step Pyramid required Imhotep to communicate precisely, use impeccable mathematics, and have excellent project management skills. This was a task with multiple parts, each complicated, each carefully orchestrated, and Imhotep accomplished it all.

Imhotep's legacy didn't end with the incredible Step Pyramid. It was only one of his notable firsts. He was also described as "the first figure of a physician to stand out clearly from the mists of antiquity" by Sir William Osler, a physician and a founder of Johns Hopkins Hospital. In his spare time Imhotep wrote the oldest known manual of surgery. The copy Imhotep himself wrote is lost, but fortunately it was recopied several times. The earliest copy ever found dates to 2500 BCE, nearly two centuries after Imhotep lived. Since then, it has been copied over and over across the centuries. In it, Imhotep describes over ninety anatomical terms, such as the heart, liver, blood vessels, and the first known descriptions of the meninges, which are the parts of the skull that surround the spinal cord and brain. It details forty-eight medical cases and the treatments that he prescribed for each of those patients. His manual explains how to suture wounds, make splints for broken bones, use bandages, apply honey as a natural disinfectant, use cannabis resin for infections, and immobilize patients to minimize the damage from lower limb fractures and spinal cord injuries. These practices have survived more than four thousand years, and some, like using splints and immobilizing spinal injuries, are still standard medical procedure today.

Imhotep is also credited with diagnosing and treating over two hundred diseases, including tuberculosis, arthritis, and appendicitis. He extracted medicines from plants, finding uses for them that are still medically relevant. His prescription for a laxative included castor oil and celery. He used saffron to treat rheumatism, acacia for coughs, and aloe to heal the skin. These ingredients can all be found in prescriptions for treating these same ailments today.

It's clear from his medical writings that Imhotep was interested in teaching future doctors. His genius left a lasting impression, and the esteem he was held in only grew to a grander scale after his death. One hundred years after his passing people began to call him a medical demigod. His skill as a writer made him a patron of scribes (another word for writer), so much so that scribes would begin the work of hand-copying texts or writing poetry by first pouring out some water from their jugs in honor of Imhotep. His fame reached its peak during 484–425 BCE, when the ill and infirm came from near and far to the banks of the Nile River to pray that Imhotep, who was now considered a full-fledged god, would prescribe treatments to heal them while they slept on the banks.

Imhotep's skill as vizier eventually earned him another godlike honor: people called him the son of Ptah, who was the chief god of Memphis, and Sekhmet, the goddess of war and pestilence.

Imhotep lived two thousand years before the birth of Hippocrates, the Greek man who has been called the father of medicine. However, it's clear that if Hippocrates is the father of medicine, Imhotep is medicine's grandfather, and he was much more than a medical genius.

An inscription on a statue of Djoser calls Imhotep

THE PRINCE OF PEACE

CHANCELLOR OF THE KING OF LOWER EGYPT

FIRST ONE UNDER THE KING

ADMINISTRATOR OF THE GREAT MANSION

HEREDITARY NOBLE

HIGH PRIEST OF HELIOPOLIS

CHIEF SCULPTOR

CHIEF CARPENTER

Though born a commoner, through sheer genius and skill, Imhotep became all these things and more, including architect, physician, dentist, and god.

METAL BONDS

While Egypt thrived, exciting discoveries in metals were being made in different parts of Africa. In the central and southern regions of the continent, copper mines began to flourish. There were small mines along the equator, the Bembe mine in Angola (modern Nigeria), mines in what is now known as the Transvaal region of South Africa, and mines in what would become Zimbabwe, Mauritania, and Niger. Africans prized copper, which they called "red gold," above actual gold because it was rarer. Copper was hammered flat, stretched into thread, and twisted into jewelry. Copper was worked and worn and became a status symbol in several different African cultures. People wore it wound around their wrists and necks and fused it with the edges and hilts of their swords as decoration. But it was gold that would change Africa. By 2400 BCE, Egypt was using gold, and that gold came to them from all over Africa, via their southern neighbor, Kush. It was gold, with its malleable nature, bright color, and rust-resistant properties, that ultimately captured the imagination of Egyptians, who believed in immortality. Their religion hinged on survival beyond death, and that made durable gold the perfect metal for their gods.

From the interior of the continent, gold moved down the

Nile into Egypt, where it was melted, hammered, and poured onto every object that would accompany a royal, the living embodiment of gods, into the afterlife: on bowls, cups, jewelry, even doorways and walls. Gold also covered the death masks and sarcophagi of the mummified remains of the royals themselves, bathing them in gleaming metal for the next life, giving them an unblemished, everlasting skin.

A millennium later, around 1000 BCE, as people were firing ceramics in the lush forests of central Africa, they found an interesting by-product in the clay. Hard, strong, and malleable, this castoff from making ceramics would change the civilizations in these forested regions. It was iron. Pottery making and iron smelting were so closely related that it was said the potter was married to the ironsmith.

The first evidence of iron smelting is from the Lake Chad region in central Africa. In the thick forests surrounding Lake Chad, hunting and trapping societies had flourished for millennia. They followed game and lived off the wild land. But after iron was discovered, the societies began to change, choosing instead to stay in one place. They became farmers, staying on the same land season after season, planting crops like barley, sorghum, and yams. In the off seasons, they specialized in finding iron beneath the soil.

Iron smelting, which extracts the metal from ore or natural rocks, is a difficult process, involving precise heating techniques, well-built furnaces, and the technology and skill to manipulate the metal into tools. Prospecting, mining, smelting, smithing, and distributing iron soon became skills as important as hunting, trapping, and farming. Iron was made into knives and swords, tools for working the soil and harvesting crops, and jewelry that showed the status of the wearer in much the same way that copper did.

As it grew in importance as a resource, iron took on a cultural importance, too, associated with abundance, birth, and power. Iron became a family business. Unlike the patrilineal descent of the kings, iron-making skills were passed down through matrilineal lines. An ironworker would teach his sisters' sons the skills of working iron, and these sons in turn would teach their own nephews.

Ironworking spread to central Nigeria by 900 BCE and to the Dogon people of Mali by 700 BCE. Metal bound societies together and separated them from others. With communities focused on what was in the ground, borders became paramount. With borders came border disputes. These disputes sometimes escalated to war, fought using the very metal that was being excavated from the soil. And as land was gained and lost, empires and kingdoms formed, fell, and rose again. In central and southern Africa, societies built on iron jostled for power and dominion. The outcome was bloody skirmishes, prisoners of war who might be killed or sold as slaves, and malleable borders that changed again and again. And so those such as the Bantu-speaking people in the middle of Africa moved, bringing their beliefs and customs to new lands, spreading their skills and ideas about metalwork, religion, and their language widely across the continent and beyond.

NATURE AS CHARACTER

Africans became careful observers of the natural world around them. They learned how to read the land, becoming adept at coaxing crops from the soil, harnessing the trees and shrubs to their advantage, and identifying where in the landscape they would find minerals like copper, iron, and gold. Careful observation of animals also told them when it was a good time to hunt and when they should leave certain animals alone. This close relationship with the land and animals may have led Africans to believe that they were communicating with the natural world. They could be given what they needed or, if they didn't follow the rules, left empty-handed.

Stories across the continent gave voice to nature—literally. People believed animals, insects, trees, and plants could talk, and that they often had more power than people. Crossing them had dire consequences. In the story "Tale of an Old Woman," a poor woman went to cut wood in the forest, hoping to sell it for food. When the tree complained, the woman explained she was alone and had no one to care for her. The tree offered her the flowers from its branches, which turned into dutiful and helpful children. It only asked that the woman never scold them. The woman lived happily with her flower children for years, until the day she scolded the youngest child for asking for something to eat. All the flower children left and returned to the tree, leaving the woman to live out her days alone and in poverty.

In the story "The King's Daughter who Lost her Hair," a young man went on a quest on behalf of a princess who had lost her long, beautiful hair. A bird asked for a lock of hair for its nest, and when the princess refused, the bird cursed her. The young man traveled far and met talking animals and even talking trees before he met the same bird who had cursed the princess. Because the prince was kind, the bird led him to the source of a cure for the princess.

These stories came from a belief in animism, the idea that plants, animals, and other natural objects have their own souls. With talking animals, plants, and even rocks, the tales were wondrous and fantastic, and they often had an underlying message. Kindness, cleverness, fairness, and using simple common sense were some of the more popular themes. Creation stories featured animals that had incredible powers, even the power to be go-betweens for people and the gods, or between the living and the ancestral and spirit worlds. Animals served as guides, as messengers, or as tricksters whose cunning often outwitted humans and other animals.

These stories took the form of proverbs, cautionary tales, and trickster tales. Trickster tales in particular became extremely popular. They were clever, amusing, and had a distinct form in which the listener to the tale was left waiting for just what maneuver would get the trickster off the hook this time. The most popular of these tricksters was the spider god, Kwaku Anansi. But even he wasn't victorious every time. Often trickster tales had a moral. In many cases it was to be cautious of gifts, or to listen to instructions carefully, but sometimes it was about the perils of greed and dishonesty. It was by these stories that African culture was exported to the rest of the world, though through terrible circumstances.

As kingdoms built on iron clashed, the people caught in between were treated as commodities to be traded. People sold into slavery took their culture, their beliefs, their stories, and their artistic techniques with them, spreading African culture to wherever they ended up. One of the most famous of these enslaved people was a man named Aesop.

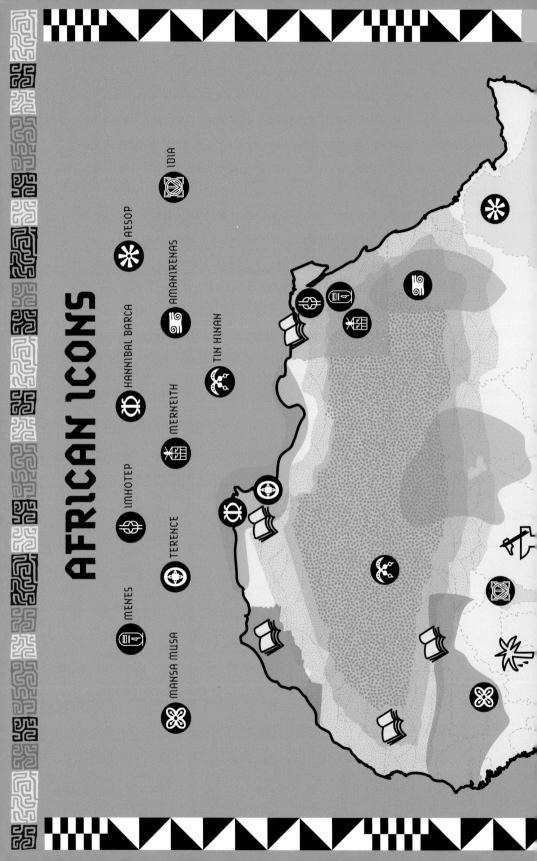

AFRICAN ICONS

MANSA MUSA

MENES

TERENCE

IMHOTEP

HANNIBAL BARCA

AESOP

MERNEITH

AMANIRENAS

TIN HINAN

IDIA

ANCIENT
LIBRARIES

EARLIEST
PALM OIL

EARLIEST
POISON

EARLIEST
IRONWORKING

EARLIEST
BOW + ARROW

EARLIEST
KNIVES

LUSH SAHARA
8500–5300 BCE

CHANGING SAHARA
5300–3500 BCE

DRY, MODERN-DAY SAHARA
3500 BCE–PRESENT

KINGDOM OF EGYPT
3200 BCE–30BCE (CAPITAL: MEMPHIS)

KINGDOM OF KUSH
1070 BCE–400 CE (CAPITAL: MEROE)

ETHIOPIA
ESTABLISHED 980 BCE

CARTHAGE
814 BCE–146 BCE

TAFILALET (MODERN-DAY MOROCCO)
757 BCE–1363 CE

KINGDOM OF BENIN
C.1200 CE–1897 CE (CAPITAL: EDO, NOW BENIN CITY)

KINGDOM OF MALI
1230 CE– C.550 CE (CAPITAL: NAINI;
ALSO TIMBUKTU, GAO, JENNE, KOUMBI SALEH)

LAKE CHAD BASIN

MODERN-DAY AFRICAN COUNTRIES

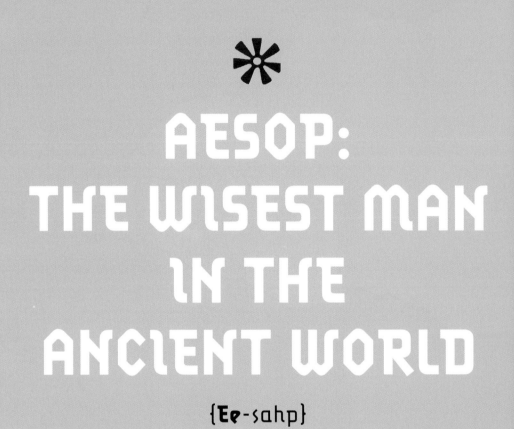

AESOP: THE WISEST MAN IN THE ANCIENT WORLD

{Ee-sahp}

The fable writer Aesop, who lived c. 620–560 BCE, was most likely an Ethiopian. He brought animist tales to the wider world when he was enslaved and taken to Greece as the property of a man named Iadmon. For the rest of his life, Aesop lived on the island of Samos, Greece, just north of the Mediterranean on the Aegean Sea.

In several accounts, Aesop is cruelly described as being small and ugly, perhaps even deformed. But his tales of animal hijinks delighted the Greek community in which he found himself working as a slave. Perhaps as a result, Aesop did not remain enslaved. It's unclear just when or how he was able to gain his freedom, but the story traditions he brought with him from Africa were likely his path out of bondage.

Aesop's fables gained popularity for expressing universal wisdoms in a simple, straightforward, and generally quite short format. His stories often showcased a small animal besting a more powerful creature through perseverance and cunning. In the story "The Eagle and the Beetle," for example, a disgruntled beetle overcomes an eagle who doesn't follow basic rules of hospitality. Aesop's trickster stories typically upend the balance of power between creatures, making the strong look like fools. Often his stories show people being foolish and the powerful abusing their position.

However, it seems that Aesop's fables might have angered some of the people who knew his work. Because some powerful people believed that his stories were a commentary on Greek life and politics, they appear to have sought revenge in an unusual and cruel way. In one story, Aesop was accused of stealing a gold cup from the temple to the god Apollo at Delphi, one of the most famous and revered temples in the ancient world.

As punishment, he was chased down and tossed from the cliffs to his death.

Even if this story is true, Aesop's accusers weren't able to put an end to the popularity of his works. His reputation and his stories lived on. The Greek historian Plutarch wrote about Aesop in his account of the Symposium of the Seven Sages after the turn of the millennium, 600 years after Aesop's death. Some believe that a chapter in the Qur'an refers to Aesop as a well-known person in Arabia. The very first recorded Cinderella story, an Egyptian myth titled "The Girl with the Rose-Red Slippers," refers to Aesop as a character who lived in Samos, Greece. Another Greek writer, Aristophanes, referred to Aesop's work in his comedy *The Wasps*, which was first staged in 422 BCE. The philosopher Plato wrote that Socrates, also a philosopher, used Aesop's fables to amuse himself while he was in jail in 399 BCE.

Over two hundred years after his death, the first anthology of Aesop's stories appeared. This was rewritten by Demetrius of Phaleron around 320 BCE as *Assemblies of Aesopic Tales.* Since then, Aesop's fables have been rewritten countless times. They were translated into Latin, distributed throughout Europe, and eventually became one of the very first books printed in English.

In the nineteenth century, in Victorian England, publishers changed Aesop's words a little to soften the shock value of some of the stories, and they simply didn't print others that were too violent for their taste. These milder versions of Aesop's fables were used to teach children to read. Aesop's stories and their morals became permanently linked to English culture and language and are still read by children today throughout the Western world. After all this time it seems that the moral in one of Aesop's most famous stories, "The Tortoise and the Hare," was right all along—slow and steady does win the race.

The Eagle and the Beetle, An Aesop Fable

A hungry eagle chased down a hare, hoping for a tasty meal. The hare, terrified and desperate, ran into a beetle's nest and begged the beetle to help him. The beetle obliged. He came out of his nest, went to the eagle, and asked him, in the name of Jupiter, to not be so inhospitable as to eat his guest, the hare. But the eagle rudely swatted the beetle away with his wing, seized the hare from the nest, and devoured him on the spot.

The eagle flew back to his* own nest, and the beetle flew after him. He intended to get his revenge. When the eagle flew away again, the beetle went to the nest and rolled the eagle's eggs out, one by one, and broke them. The eagle was enraged and puzzled as to who would do such a thing. He moved his nest to a higher place. Again, the beetle flew there and broke the eggs, exactly as he had done before.

At a loss for what to do, the eagle flew up to Jupiter and begged the god to keep his eggs safe. He put the eggs in Jupiter's lap, certain this would work. But again, the beetle followed. He made a ball of dirt and threw it into Jupiter's lap. The god hopped up, and so the eggs fell and broke a third time.

The beetle then informed Jupiter about the eagle's inhospitality and went on his way. When the eagle returned,

Jupiter explained that it had been the beetle all along who had been breaking the eagle's eggs and explained why he agreed with the beetle. However, he didn't want all the eagle's eggs to be destroyed, so he asked the beetle to make peace with the eagle and put the matter to rest.

The beetle refused.

The only thing left for Jupiter to do was change the eagle's breeding season to a different time of year, when there are no beetles out and about.

Moral: *No one can slight the laws of hospitality and get away with it without consequence; and there is no one who is powerful or influential enough to protect the oppressor from the vengeance of the oppressed.*

*You may have noticed that all of the characters in the story are male. It's interesting that most of the characters in Aesop's fables are. But you may also notice that the eagle is protecting eggs, and has more and more eggs to protect, which suggests that the eagle is, in fact, female. Since both male and female beetles dig nests, the beetle may have been either male or female.

ACROSS
THE WAVES

Along the northern shore of the African continent, it was the sea that buoyed life in the first millennium BCE. The Mediterranean was awash with ships ferrying people, cargo, and ideas. Metal, oil, and grain moved on the waves between North African cities like Carthage (which is in modern-day Tunisia) and Greece, Rome, France, and Spain. Ivory carvings from deep in Africa were exported, along with a yellowish marble with streaks of pink, red, and green that was quarried near Carthage.

Goods didn't only leave Africa—they were also brought in. The Phoenicians, seafaring merchants from West Asia, brought a dye made of murex shells. Its color was so remarkable and so rare that it became the color of European royalty: purple. Ideas from abroad also came to Africa. The Phoenicians' writing system was further developed by the Greeks. It eventually became the alphabet we know today. The Greek style of architecture, sculpture, and literature influenced the cultures of every shore the Mediterranean touched. The city of Carthage used Greek columns and sculptures in their architecture.

The first millennium BCE was a time when African, Asian, and European cultures were freely mingling because of their access to each other via the sea.

But the sea also brought war to Africa. The Phoenicians, driven by a desire to expand their trading posts, conquered Carthage, making it their main post. They took the city by force and pushed the indigenous Africans out of their homelands. Then, in an audacious move, they hired the Africans to be their military.

Thanks to the efforts of the Phoenicians, Carthage had become the most prosperous sea town in North Africa. Just 368 miles across the Mediterranean Sea from Rome, and within sailing distance along the northern edge of Africa to Spain, Carthaginian ships dominated the waters and bravely ventured into the Atlantic, beyond the edge of the known world. Their empire stretched all along the northern border of Africa from what is now Tunisia, in both directions: west and north into Spain, and east and south into land that is now occupied by modern-day Libya, and reaching toward Egypt. The Carthaginians also occupied most of Sicily, as well as all the islands in the middle of the Mediterranean: the Balearic Islands, Sardinia, and Corsica. They accumulated great wealth and attracted the ire of Rome.

Roman forays across the Mediterranean frustrated the Carthaginians. Roman military maneuvers delayed or outright stopped merchant ships. In addition, Roman forces attempted to conquer every port along the Mediterranean Sea. One main port of contention was Sicily. Rome didn't like Carthage having a toehold in a city that was so close by. Carthage and Rome fought over the land, and they finally agreed that Sicily was the domain of Carthage. But this didn't stop Rome from eyeing Carthage and its riches.

HANNIBAL BARCA: UNPARALLELED MILITARY STRATEGIST

{**Han**-uh-buhl **Bahr**-kuh}

annibal Barca hated Rome. Most Carthaginians did. When he was born in 247 BCE, the Phoenicians' grip on trade and wealth in North Africa was beginning to slip. The fledgling Roman Empire was only too happy to step in, and they did so with military might. The First Punic War (264–241 BCE) was a conflict between the two Mediterranean powers and was fought on land and on sea. The fighting had already been raging on for nearly twenty years when infant Hannibal was born, and the conflict with Rome would shape Hannibal's life.

Hannibal's father, Hamilcar Barca, was the general of the Carthaginian armies during the First Punic War. When the war ended, it was agreed that Carthage was to hold on to its lands, but pay tributes to Rome. Despite the end of the war, though, the two cities still clashed. As a child, Hannibal was taught what it meant to have a mortal enemy. When he was about nine years old, his father took him to one of the victims of war, likely a Roman soldier. He put Hannibal's hand on the dead body and made him swear that Rome would forever be his enemy. Hannibal swore the oath.

By his father's side for years on the battlefield against Rome, Hannibal learned how to track enemies and was trained in hand-to-hand combat and military strategy. But perhaps most importantly, Hannibal learned how to lead. After Hamilcar drowned, and the next general was assassinated seven years later, the troops unanimously elected Hannibal to be their new general. He was just twenty-five years old.

By 218 BCE, when he was twenty-nine, Hannibal had had enough of Rome's incessant encroachment on the agreements that had ended the First Punic War. When Rome installed a new government that was opposed to Carthage in the Spanish city of Saguntum, Hannibal vowed to do something about it. He brought the full strength of his army, Carthage's alliance with Spain, and his own keen strategy to the undertaking. He gathered his troops and took them on foot through North Africa to cross the thin strip of sea that separated Africa from Spain. His troops laid siege to the Roman-held city of Saguntum and took it. Rome was furious. They demanded that Hannibal be handed over to them. When the senators of Carthage refused, the Second Punic War began.

Rather than returning home to fight the Romans in Carthage, Hannibal decided to meet the Romans on their home turf. In an unprecedented move, and certainly one no one could have anticipated, he marched with the Carthaginian troops toward the Alps, a mountain range with snowy peaks and thin rocky passes. As Hannibal went, he liberated towns from the grip of the Romans and made new allies, and in so doing, he amassed more and more troops. By the time he reached the Alps, he had fifty thousand troops on the ground and nine thousand in cavalry. In addition, he had at least thirty-seven war elephants from Africa.

The terrain of the Alps would have presented difficulties for anyone. Add to that hostile residents throwing huge rocks in the way of the Carthaginian army, and it seemed like Hannibal's strategy was bound to fail. The toll was steep. After seventeen days, Hannibal emerged from the Alps with only twenty-six thousand troops of the nearly sixty thousand he had begun with and just a few elephants. None of this deterred Hannibal, however. He led his army down the mountain and through the south of France toward Italy.

The stunning move surprised Roman General Scipio Africanus, who was also a young military leader, in his early thirties at the time. He met Hannibal in northern Italy, only to be dealt several defeats by Hannibal's sparser, more tired, and less equipped troops. The war elephants were something Roman troops had never seen before. Huge, armored, and with up to four soldiers riding on top, they were almost undefeatable. Hannibal had a habit of riling up the elephants before battle, making them angry so they would attack anything in their path. The Romans were entirely unprepared.

It was diplomacy and strategy that ultimately gave Hannibal the upper hand, though, not military might. Hannibal didn't really have the means to defeat Scipio. He had been forced to leave vital war supplies behind on the Spanish side of the Alps. The troops were living off what they could find wherever they were, and there were very few of them left compared to Scipio's army. So Hannibal decided not to take cities in northern Italy by force. Just as he had when he passed through the Spanish side of the Alps, he offered himself up as a liberator, freeing the people from Roman oppression. As a result, people joined his side, and his army once again grew.

Hannibal won victory after victory against the Romans, often using natural elements against them. At Lake Trasimene, for example, his army drove the Romans into the water, drowning fifteen thousand of them. By the winter of 216–215 BCE he had retreated to Capua. He and his men had been fighting for years with no support from Carthage. His requests for supplies went unheard by Carthaginian senators. Roman spies infiltrated his troops with orders to assassinate Hannibal. So the general took to wearing disguises, including wigs. Even people who knew him well could not recognize him when he was in one of his costumes.

When spring came, the Romans set a trap for Hannibal. The Carthaginian troops were penned in, with a river on one side and the Roman army waiting on the other. One night, the Romans saw lights coming down toward where they had the most troops. The Roman general Fabius Verrucosus was sure Hannibal couldn't break through at that location. He was right. Hannibal couldn't do it. In the morning, Verrucosus sent the rest of his troops to that place to aid in what he expected would be a slaughter of the Carthaginian army. The only problem was—there was no army. Only cows. Hannibal and his men had tied torches to the horns of cattle and sent them toward the Roman stronghold. When Verrucosus moved the rest of his troops there to fight Hannibal, Hannibal and his men slipped through the pass the Romans left unattended.

The next battle would be at Cannae in southeastern Italy. Another set of Roman military leaders came at Hannibal with a force of fifty thousand to Hannibal's thirty thousand, which was cobbled together from those who had joined his campaign against Rome. Thoroughly outmanned, Hannibal only had strategy on his side. He set up his troops in a crescent with the weakest point at the middle and his strongest cavalry on the outer edges. He knew the Roman troops were stronger in the middle. He also pushed them into a wedge with a hill on one side and the river on the other. He made sure they were facing a hot, dusty wind that irritated their eyes. As the Romans pushed through the middle, Hannibal's men fell back, allowing the cavalry on the outer edges to surround the Romans. Then they moved in. The strategy was very successful. Of the original fifty thousand Roman troops, only fourteen thousand escaped, while ten thousand were captured. The others were all killed. Hannibal's losses were considerably fewer, with only six thousand men dead.

After Cannae, only one Roman general was willing to face

Hannibal: Scipio. And luck was on his side. After eight years of fighting, Hannibal, though seemingly undefeatable in battle, had few supplies, and support from the cities he had tried to liberate was waning. In 205 BCE, Scipio allied himself with Masinissa, an African king from Numidia, a Berber kingdom in what is now Algeria and part of Tunisia. The Numidians had been allies of Carthage, so losing any support from them put the city in direct danger. In 203 BCE, Hannibal quit Italy to help his homeland. By 202 BCE, Scipio was ready to meet Hannibal on his home turf of Carthage.

Hannibal was sure he would be able to confound Scipio using his war elephants, but this time, it didn't work. After the Romans' initial encounter with the elephants, Scipio was prepared. The Roman troops quickly killed the war elephants' handlers, then turned the animals on the Carthaginian troops. Hannibal was finally defeated. The war was over.

The fighting, which had lasted for seventeen years, affected every person in Carthage and Rome. No one was left without an opinion of the war. One Roman senator, Cato the Elder, made a habit of ending all of his speeches—regardless of what the speech was about—with the line: "Further, I think that Carthage should be destroyed."

Hannibal was made the chief magistrate of a defeated Carthage, which had to pay tribute to Rome. The Romans also continually asked for Hannibal to be turned over to them. The only one who refused to call for Hannibal's head was his rival Scipio. His former enemy very much respected Hannibal as a general and refused to have him captured and brought to Rome. For this, the Romans called Scipio a traitor. At the same time, the Carthaginian senators who had refused to send Hannibal any aid now accused him of betrayal. Hannibal knew that if he stayed at home it was only a matter of time before he would have to face Rome. So he decided to leave his beloved Carthage in 195 BCE for Tyre in what is now Lebanon, on the east coast of the Mediterranean Sea. There he served as a consultant to King Antiochus III. Despite Hannibal's many victories in battle, the king was wary of putting him in charge of land troops and instead gave him a naval vessel. Hannibal, so successful on land, floundered at sea. In 189 BCE, Antiochus was defeated by the Romans, and Hannibal knew his time was up. Rather than be handed over to his enemy, he drank poison, saying, "Let us put an end to this life, which has caused so much dread to the Romans." He was sixty-five years old, and the promise he had made to his father as a young boy to never be a friend to the Romans remained fulfilled.

Hannibal's smart use of mobile units, strategic leadership of a small number of men against a larger army, bold maneuvers (like crossing the Alps in winter), and effective deployment of cavalry to envelop and trap the enemy are some of his strategies that were studied long after his death. Hannibal also used natural elements to his advantage. In addition to using cows to fool the Romans, he also forced their troops to cross a frozen river and used fog to hide his men. What Scipio learned from fighting Hannibal was adopted by the Romans. It fueled their eventual domination in the region. Military leaders from King Charlemagne, who ruled from 768 to 814; to Napoleon Bonaparte, the emperor of France (1804–1814); to United States military leader General Patton, who commanded the Seventh Army during World War II (1939–1945), all studied and used Hannibal's methods.

TERENCE: NORTH AFRICAN PLAYWRIGHT

{Tair-ihnts}

Even after being defeated by Scipio, and despite having to pay out huge sums as a result, the Carthage of 170 BCE was still beautiful. Built from nearly nothing about two hundred years earlier, it remained busy with trade and was fortified and protected by an impressive navy. The city was a study in extremes. The wealthiest people, who ran the city and gave it its culture, lived in grand palaces close to the central markets. Many had rural homes far from the city, where they could retire in the summer heat. An underclass of enslaved people took care of the business of cleaning, cooking, building, and all manner of physical labor, with little hope of ever reaching the level of slaveholders in society, even if they did eventually win back their freedom. It was in this city that a young man who would come to influence literature for centuries lived.

He was known as Terentius Publius Afer, or Terence, a name given to him by the man who bought him in Carthage and took him to Rome. This man was the senator P. Terentius Lucanus. The senator immediately named Terence after himself and added "Afer" as a reference to Terence's home continent. Whatever his birth family called him when he was born, history doesn't know, and Terence himself seems to have shed his original name with the city he was forced to leave behind.

Terence was an impressive storyteller, and this caught Lucanus' attention. The senator saw to Terence's education and then freed him. Terence used the opportunity to enter fully into the Roman literary scene. Other writers of the time included Plautus, who wrote Greek comedies, and Ennius, who became known as the "father of Latin poetry." Terence, Plautus, and Ennius emerged as the major literary figures of Rome, working in the popular style of taking older Greek comedies and rewriting them for a Roman audience.

These kinds of Greek plays were considered to be the highest form of literature at the time. Many writers thought it was best to remain as faithful as possible to the originals. Terence did not. He eliminated lengthy opening speeches that explained the whole plot, so that when the audience was watching, the events and twists would be unexpected and more exciting. Terence also focused more on developing characters and dialogue than on the jokes. He took creative liberty with the original material. He might combine plot points or characters from different original plays into new ones. In his very first work, *Andria* (166 BCE), Terence incorporated material from another play called *Perinthia*. His fourth play, *Eunuchus* (161 BCE), benefitted from the addition of two characters from another play, *Kolax*.

Rome's elite class loved what he did. A famed actor named Lucius Ambivius Turpio also took an interest in Terence's work, and he helped to promote his career. Though Turpio was old by the time he and Terence met, he still had enough influence to help the young playwright become successful.

Terence may have been a darling of the elite class, but some of his fellow writers didn't admire his work. Another playwright of the time, Luscius Lanuvinus, started a campaign against Terence, saying that his hybrid plays used lesser works that contaminated Greek masterpieces. The fact that Terence seamlessly mixed plays and wrote with skill was no comfort to Lanuvinus. For people who believed Greek art to be the pinnacle of culture, the way he wrote his plays was a serious offense.

Despite his rival's campaign against his work, Terence's

play *Eunuchus* was so successful that there were several performances, which earned Terence a lot of money. But like all artists, not all of his plays were successful. His second one, called *Hecyra*, failed twice. Both times it was because there was more enticing entertainment available on performance days. The first time it was performed, the audience left because they heard there were a tightrope walker and boxers nearby. The second time, audience members abandoned the performance to see gladiators who were fighting nearby.

In addition to the jealous rivals, there were also rumors that Terence wasn't the real writer of his work and that other people wrote the plays for him. None of these accusations or rumors was ever seriously considered, and they certainly didn't reduce Terence's popularity in his own time.

In all, Terence wrote six plays between 166 and 160 BCE. Each one of them was an adaptation of older Greek comedies, but because of how original his writing was, his work has been held up as a model of pure Latin, and it started a new form of comedy called the comedy of manners. This style pokes fun at contemporary society and culture, especially making fun of the behavior of the upper class.

Terence's plays remained popular hundreds of years later, during the Middle Ages and the Renaissance. His simple and direct writing style may have made for their lasting appeal. For centuries after his passing, Terence's works were copied over and over again by scribes and others trying to learn Latin. He influenced modern writers like American playwright Thornton Wilder, who based his novel *The Woman of Andros* on Terence's first play, *Andria.* Even U.S. president John Adams thought his writing was "remarkable" and that it should be studied.

On a trip to Greece, Terence disappeared. He was either twenty-five or thirty-five. He may have died at sea, or on his way back to Rome, or perhaps he simply chose not to return. Like his birth, his death remains uncertain. But the plays that he wrote in his short time as a playwright made a lasting impact on literature.

AMANIRENAS: WARRIOR, DIPLOMAT, QUEEN

{Ah-man-ih-**ray**-nus}

Around 40 BCE, the Kingdom of Kush was a civilization as well developed as Egypt, with centralized cities, pyramids to bury their dead, and a system of government with a queen or king at the head. Unlike Egypt, it was thick with trees, and beneath Kushite soil were rich iron deposits and soft gold. Kush was happy to trade these luxuries to their northern neighbor Egypt. Wood, iron, and gold were transported down the Nile. The wood was used to make Egyptian buildings and craft their barges; gold covered the royals in a metal that would never tarnish; and Kushite iron was used in everything, from tools to weapons, that would be wielded by Egyptian hands.

The weapons were increasingly necessary. After centuries of peaceful trade with the Romans and Arabic nations, Egypt's abundant grains, beautiful cities, and invasion-resistant borders became coveted throughout the region. Peoples across the Mediterranean and Asia wanted to conquer them. The Romans were successful in taking over Egypt, thanks in large part to the military tactics they had learned from General Hannibal of Carthage. The last Egyptian dynasty, which was the thirty-second, collapsed with the death by suicide of its final pharaoh, Cleopatra, in 30 BCE.

By 29 BCE, Egypt was totally under Roman control. Caesar Augustus, the emperor of Rome and head of the Roman army, ruled. He made Egypt a Roman province and left Cornelius Gallus in charge as its prefect. Rome's elite troops were sent to protect Egypt, which quickly was nicknamed "Rome's breadbasket." As Rome grew, the surrounding areas became incapable of providing enough food for their people. Egypt was a necessary acquisition. With Egypt secured, Caesar Augustus turned his attention farther south, to Kush and its abundant wood, iron, and gold. Controlling both Egypt and Kush would mean food and wealth for Rome. Augustus may have believed that conquering Kush would be easy compared to the campaigns the Romans had waged to gain Egypt. Kush was a much smaller kingdom, and the Romans believed the Kushite leaders were weak. On the latter point, they were very wrong. The kingdom was led by Amanirenas, who was fierce in battle, cunning in strategy, and undeniably skilled in diplomacy.

Amanirenas was kandake of Kush from about 40 BCE. "Kandake" (also spelled "candace") meant queen or queen mother. Kandakes could rule alone at a time when no other country in the world had female rulers. Even Egypt's queen regents were only placeholders for future kings. Kandake Amanirenas ruled alongside her husband, King Teriteqas. By all accounts they were equals both on the throne and in battle. It was not unusual for Amanirenas to ride into skirmishes with her husband and fight at his side.

The Kushite royalty were well aware of Cleopatra's death and the fall of Egypt. The pharaoh's children had been sent south toward Ethiopia*, where Cleopatra hoped an Ethiopian queen would care for them. However, the children never made it that far. The people of Kush knew Caesar Augustus was looking to expand south. Augustus demanded taxes and tribute from Kush and kept attempting to push Egypt's border farther south. Skirmishes between Roman Egypt and Kush left the border in constant contest. Fortunately, the Kushites also knew that Rome had other border problems. Arabian troops were marching on Roman lands. It was just the distraction Kush needed. In 24 BCE, after five years of fighting at the border shared by Egypt and Kush, Caesar Augustus had to turn his attention to a campaign in Arabia. Amanirenas and Teriteqas used the opportunity to strategize about the best way to protect their kingdom.

When the Egyptian prefect, Cornelius Gallus, left Egypt with a portion of his troops, Amanirenas and her husband saw their chance. They mounted a preemptive attack against Roman Egypt. The king and queen rode north with their army, bringing the fight to the Egyptian cities of Syene and Philae. The attacks were a surprise to the Romans, but Roman troops were disciplined and deadly. They struck back. Not content to sit on the sidelines calling the shots, both Amanirenas and Teriteqas fought in the thick of the battle. In one of their early clashes, the king was fatally wounded. Undaunted, Amanirenas had her son Akinidad join her on the battlefield. Together they led their army to victory, destroying the cities of Syene and Philae. They took prisoners and defaced statues that Augustus had erected to himself as they went. Victorious and defiant, Amanirenas had the prisoners of war fed to her pet lion. It was a brutal end, but one that sent a clear message to Rome that she was not to be trifled with.

Amanirenas had several Roman statues sent back to Kush as souvenirs, including one large bronze head of Caesar which she had cut off from the rest of the statue. Amanirenas ordered that the head should be buried under the steps of a temple dedicated to victory so that people coming and going, and the kandake herself, would constantly walk over it.

The Roman governor, Gaius Petronius, retaliated after the kandake's attack. He amassed ten thousand men and eight hundred horses. Once again, the queen rode to face the Roman troops. Once again, she fought in the thick of the battle. This time, in close combat, she lost an eye for her efforts. The injury didn't stop her. But afterward Petronius began to refer to her as the "one-eyed kandake."

After this attack, Amanirenas and Petronius attempted peace talks in the city of Dakka on the Egyptian and Kushite border later in 24 BCE, but they were unable to reach a diplomatic solution. The fighting started up again just outside the city. This time, her son Akinidad was struck down as he fought alongside the Kushite troops. He was taken away from the battle and into the city to be cared for, but his wounds were fatal.

Amanirenas and her troops fell back. The losses were perhaps too brutal to bear.

By 22 BCE Petronius had pushed his troops deeper into the kingdom. Eventually they reached the capital, Napata, and destroyed it. It was the residence of the kandake, and losing it was a devastating blow. Thousands of Kushites were sold into slavery. Petronius moved farther south. He and his army installed forts on Kush land. But if he had hoped the move would force the kandake to concede defeat, he was mistaken. Amanirenas sought support from neighboring countries in southern and central Africa. When she turned once again to fight the Romans, she had at her command an unmatched army of archers, infantry, and war elephants that could best any of the Roman horses with sheer size and ferocity. To top it off, the kandake had her lions to feed on fallen or captured enemies. The queen was unwavering in her determination to defeat the Romans. The Kush army with her at the helm must have been a spectacular and terrifying sight.

Amanirenas' army rode north to Qasr Ibrim, intending to take it back from the Romans. Petronius was alerted to the invasion and rode south to meet them. Once again, the two sides clashed. The fighting forced Rome's hand. They could not afford to lose Egypt's wheat. And without Amanirenas they were cut off from the wealth of southern and central Africa. Unable to defeat the formidable kandake, Caesar Augustus sought peace. A delegation of diplomats from Kush was given passage to talk with him in Rome.

According to an oral history, when the diplomats arrived, they presented Augustus with a set of arrows made of pure gold. They told him that if he was interested in peace, the arrows were a gift from their queen as a token of her warmth and friendship. If he wanted war, however, he should keep the arrows, because he would need them.

Amanirenas negotiated the Romans' retreat out of Kush, got Augustus to rescind his order to tax the Kushites, had the Romans help to rebuild the buildings and temples they had destroyed, and agreed that the Kushites would have free passage to Egyptian temples since some of their people believed in many of the same gods. In the face of everything, Amanirenas would maintain the pride of Kush. But that wasn't all. Kush would now trade with the Romans and carry on the already existing trade agreements with Roman Egypt. It was quite a coup for Kush, given that the Romans were already entrenched inside the Kushite kingdom. How did she do it? The Kushite part of the history, written in their own language of Meroitic script, is still yet to be deciphered. The answers are there, in their own words. Until then, we can only surmise that Amanirenas was as skillful at negotiating as she was at battle.

As a show of good faith, Amanirenas returned to the Romans some of the statuary that she and her forces had taken at Philae. She did not return all of the pieces, however. The bronze head of Caesar Augustus remained beneath the stairs of the temple, where it would be trampled daily. The Romans had no idea that she had the piece, and certainly not that she was using it to insult their leader.

Amanirenas increased the wealth of her kingdom by expanding Kush's existing trade network to include Rome. Kush's strength in trade grew, and the next three kandakes benefited from Amanirenas's decisions. Each one reigned over a Kush that had more wealth than the one before. The most prosperous period came just after the turn of the millennium, when Kandake Amanitore ruled from 1 to 25 CE.

And in all that time and the years and centuries to follow, no one knew that a bronze head of Caesar Augustus lay under the ground in Kush. It was a final, lasting joke she played on the Roman emperor. The head of Augustus lay perfectly preserved, exactly where Amanirenas had it buried, until it was uncovered by an archaeologist in 1910.

A stela depicting (left to right) the goddess Amesemi, the kandake Amanishakheto, and the god Apedemak.

*The Romans referred to any land south of Egypt as "Ethiopia," so in this case, Ethiopia may have meant Kush itself and not a land farther away.

WHERE FEW DARED TO TREAD

The Kingdom of Kush was not the only place with rich mineral deposits beneath its soil. In west and central Africa, where fertile soil yielded crops like millet and cowpeas, farmers tilling the earth with hoes and rakes occasionally turned up copper and gold under their tools. Iron was discovered by accident when they fired ceramics, but as they discovered how useful it was, people soon learned how to prospect for it. They developed ways to purify the metals and work them into tools, weapons, art, and jewelry. Over centuries, purification methods improved. The farmers who learned to prospect for metals in the soil honed their skills, making metal detection a science based on experienced observation. Whole kingdoms began to develop around areas that were metal-rich. But unless they could trade those metals, whatever they found was useless. And in order to trade, they would have to cross the Sahara.

Crossing the Sahara was difficult, dangerous, and often deadly. The sands had no markers, and dunes shifted with the wind from one day to the next. Navigating over them was as difficult as tracing a path over an unknown sea. The conditions were brutal. The sun was scorching during the day; winds whipped up choking, blinding sand; and at night the temperature dropped to near freezing, and travelers could be left exposed with nowhere to turn for shelter. For those on the outskirts of the Sahara, the desert was a formidable foe, but one that needed to be conquered. There was money to be made for those who dared cross it. Many set their sights across the Sahara's pale and perilous dunes, eager for trade.

As early as 19 BCE, the Romans had begun expeditions into the desert, but these ended around 86 CE when they had made little progress navigating the sands. The Egyptians settled around the periphery of the Sahara in land rich with water and didn't bother with the desert at all. Historians over several ages wrote about it, from Strabo, who lived during the turn of the millennium, to Pliny the Elder, who lived during the first century CE, to Ptolemy, a second-century historian. All of them looked to the vast desert with wonder, but they couldn't figure out how to cross it.

However, while Romans and Egyptians scratched their heads at the insurmountable problem of the Sahara, a group of people in the north had long figured it out.

After the settlement of Carthage by the Phoenicians in 814 BCE, the Berber people, native Africans who lived in Carthage, had been displaced, then spread out across northern Africa, from Morocco in the northwest all the way to the Egyptian border. But long before they were driven from their ancestral homeland, they had established trade relationships and lines of commerce with other communities across the desert starting around 3000 BCE, during the Bronze Age, before the Sahara became as dry as we know it today. Berbers were accustomed to taking everything they owned on long desert crossings. They became a society of nomads, and they understood the desert like no others.

Scattered across the north, at the fringes of the dunes, the Berbers prepared for trading trips that would take months across ever-shifting sands on paths that only they understood. They sometimes used horses, but camels, the Berbers discovered, were better-suited to lengthy desert expeditions. Their humps stored fat that could sustain them when food and water became scarce, and they had two eyelids with long lashes to protect their eyes from the sand, as well as a third, clear eyelid to wipe the surface of the eye clean of dust. They could also carry heavy loads across great distances. The animals would be loaded with food and water for both people and animals, tents, bedding materials, weapons, cooking utensils, and, of course, goods for trade. The Berbers themselves were not as naturally suited to the desert heat as their animals, but they adapted. They wore long, loose woven clothing that kept them protected from the sun but allowed the occasional breeze to pass through. They covered their heads with long scarves, the ends of which they wrapped across their faces, like veils, to protect their noses and mouths from the sand's sharp grains. The Berbers traditionally dressed in bright colors, but were particularly fond of a brilliant shade of blue, from a dye made with the leaves of indigo plants.

At the outset of each journey, they were well aware that not everyone or everything that started out might make it to their destination. Even for the Berber people, the hazards of the desert were unpredictable. Overburdened camels might not survive the crossing, causing the Berbers to leave behind valuable supplies and goods in the sand. In spite of careful preparations, people could also succumb to the blistering heat and the lack of water. Meanwhile, other Berbers chose to be bandits, making their money through theft rather than trade, waiting to attack. There were many ways to die in the desert.

TIN HINAN: FOUNDING A CITY ON THE DUNES

{Tihn **Hih**-nan}

T in Hinan's people thrived where others found only hardship. This nomadic group of Berbers called the Tuareg had found a way to subsist within the desert for many centuries by Tin Hinan's birth in the fourth century CE. Among the dry dunes, they could find places to graze their animals. They had learned how to hunt the few animals in scrub zones just on the outskirts of the desert, like antelope and wild sheep. Spread out north and south of the desert, they traveled to trade with other Tuareg groups, always shifting with the sands, never staying in any one place for long. Their tents of dyed red animal skins and all their belongings could be packed up in a moment.

Perhaps more than others of her people, Tin Hinan was used to adapting to difficulties. A deformity of her spine forced her to walk with a limp, and never without the assistance of a walking stick, but by all accounts she was a fierce warrior, and her disability didn't deter her from lofty goals. Tin Hinan means "she of the tents" and is a title rather than a proper name. Some say her real name was Tiski al-Ardja, which means either Tiski the Sweet-Smelling or Tiski the Lame.

Tin Hinan realized something important about the desert: if there was a permanent city inside the Sahara, every traveler crossing the dunes would stop there, coming or going, to seek food, shelter, rest, and protection and to replenish their supplies. So anyone who could build that city in the desert would thrive. It was a crucial time. Iron and gold from sub-Saharan regions were being turned up in the soil at an astonishing rate. So too were vast deposits of salt. On the desert's edges were people wishing to make safe crossing so that they could engage in trade with far-flung nations.

There is no record of what prompted Tin Hinan to search

for a place to settle in the desert, nor what gave her the confidence to do so. We do know that she set out from Tafilalet, in what is now Morocco, beautifully decked out with jewels, the flowing garments of her people, a single white camel, and her servant, Takamet, at her side. They traveled southeast into the Sahara and came to the Ahaggar Mountains in modern-day Algeria, where she found an oasis. Oases are rare watering holes in the desert, places where animals and people can be refreshed and a few scant plants will grow. The Tuareg were used to finding water in the desert, so this location may have already been known to Tin Hinan or others. And it may not have been the first oasis that Tin Hinan encountered on her trek, but something about it must have seemed to her the perfect spot to set up a city. She returned to her people and convinced many of them to follow her to the oasis, where they founded a city inside the Sahara.

Tin Hinan became the first Tuareg queen, and she established a matrilineal society in which wealth passed from mothers to daughters and women owned the property. When couples married, the men moved into the homes of the women. Tin Hinan placed veils on the men, colored the favorite bright blue of the Berbers. From puberty, men started covering their faces as a sign of respect to the women of their society, and they never took off their veils except in the presence of their wives. Women did not veil their faces, though they may have covered their hair for religious reasons.

The society Tin Hinan created had caste divisions, which likely survived in the caste divisions that still existed in the early twentieth century. The top caste included nobles, who saw themselves as a warrior class and claimed Tin Hinan as their ancestor. Next was a servant class that cared for goats but could not own camels, then a class of cultivators who lived permanently at oases. Teachers and artisans were each in their own separate classes beneath nobles. Those who served the nobles were at the bottom. This peasant class of the Tuareg claimed they descended from Tin Hinan's servant, Takamet.

Tin Hinan's influence stretched further than the trek she made into the desert to set up an oasis city. To this day, the Tuareg people, who still live in North and West African countries, revere women more than most societies from the continent. Though women are not involved in politics, their opinions are highly sought after, and the women's tents are the place where everyone gathers. Women also have freedoms that most other women on the continent couldn't dream of, like choosing their own mates, and even choosing when to divorce. When marriages end, the woman retains the children, the tents, all domestic animals, and communal goods. The men leave empty-handed, perhaps with only a camel to transport them back to their mother's house.

It is the stuff of legend: a disabled woman of the fourth century walking into a desert, founding a city, and becoming a queen. Centuries later, historians thought she was just that—an incredible legend—until her grave was found in 1925.

The tomb itself was a surprise. The building was Roman and was from about 19 BCE when the Romans had begun their first forays into the desert, looking for a way through. They failed and abandoned the forts they had built. But the woman who triumphed over the desert was laid to rest in one of these structures. Tin Hinan lay underground in one of the rooms, buried under nine stone slabs. Her bones were placed on a wooden platform, her legs crossed, her head tilted to the side. She was covered with a red leather cloak, which had either mostly rotted away in the desert heat or become food for the many scorpions that scurried into the shadows when her tomb once again saw the light. On her left arm were seven gold bracelets. Seven silver bracelets were worn on her right. She wore necklaces of turquoise, garnet, amazonite, and carnelian. Pottery jars surrounding her had been filled with grapes and dates to sustain her on her last journey. There was even a Roman coin of Constantine I. It was a burial befitting a queen, one whose incredible daring helped to establish a city in the desert right at the time when people needed safe haven to establish routes of trade.

Tin Hinan's entrance into the Sahara came just before the Tuareg's trans-Saharan trade route became popular. This new trade route made it possible for people from all parts of the continent, and across the world, to exchange ideas, goods, and resources, all led by the Tuareg, who became wealthy and powerful as they controlled the paths of trade. Regular crossings over the desert began in the fifth century CE, just after Tin Hinan made her way through the desert sands and established a city. Sahara crossings would soon become the most important byway of commerce in the world. It fortified the Tuareg and solidified them as a powerful presence in northern Africa, and it aided in the rise of Ghana, a new kingdom poised to grow mighty because of all the gold its people found within its borders.

ACROSS THE GOLDEN SAND

After Tin Hinan founded a city in the Sahara where those crossing the desert could rest and revive, the trans-Saharan trade route increased in popularity. Traders and explorers immediately took advantage of the opportunities that came with being able to safely (at least mostly safely) cross the desert. Caravans appeared on the horizon, their forms bending and flickering in the distance as waves of heat rose over the dunes. They were loaded with goods, ready to travel miles of crisscrossed routes. The noisy, chaotic scene would straighten out as the large caravan approached a city or another caravan.

From northern points such as Tunis, Algiers, and Tangier, traders moved into the desert with glazed ceramics, glass beads, fruits, and textiles from North Africa and the Mediterranean. Horses went south from Tripoli in Libya. Cotton and iron tools were moved west from Cairo, Egypt. In places like Takedda in Niger, Sijilmasa in Ghana, and Audaghost in Mauritania, workers chiseled slabs of salt out of the ground for a never-ending

stream of merchants. The rectangular blocks were tied to horses and camels and traded via the Saharan routes. They would be used for cooking wherever they were traded. But the most impressive source of salt according to Muslim writers of the time was Teghaza, Mali, where salt was used as building material. Towering over the city was an entire castle made of rock salt. Every room, floor, and battlement was crafted from the same salt that was being sold across the continent. Rock slabs from trading posts in Sijilmasa, Ghana, and Aoudaghost, Mauritania, moved through the desert. The Saharan trade routes crisscrossed, met, and diverged from one another, conveying goods to multiple cities along the way and from there to points beyond. Goods that began at one point could end up anywhere along the many paths through the Sahara and into the African continent.

Farther south, in sub-Saharan Africa, in mines spread across Senegal, Mali, Guinea, Burkina Faso, Côte d'Ivoire, and Ghana, there was gold. The most popular mines were the Bure on the Upper Niger River and the Bambuk in western Sudan, between the Falame and Upper Senegal. From Central and South Africa, oryx-hide shields made their way north, eventually finding their way to the Niger river to be transported and traded. Their quality was legendary. People believed that the hides, if punctured, would magically heal themselves as if nothing had ever struck them. Many of these shields ended up in Spain, held against the bodies of Spanish soldiers as they warred with invading kings.

The Berbers led the caravans for eager merchants. Everything was carefully secured on camel after camel, some animals pale as the desert sand, others dark as the men they also carried on their backs. The men rode on saddles attached to the camels' high humps, fitting their feet into the curve at the base of each camel's neck. The men's bright blue robes billowed in the wind, and their faces were veiled for protection against the hot, sharp sand, leaving only their dark eyes squinting in the sunlight, searching for dangers such as sandstorms, bandits, or wells with foul, brackish water that would make both people and animals sick—anything that might interrupt their course. Short, sharp swords on armbands flashed in the relentless sun, the handles close enough for ready hands to grab and wield. Some Berber people, such as the Lamta and the Gazula, lay in wait at popular wells with the intent to ambush those who would stop for water. Guides needed to be ever vigilant. The caravans moved slowly but steadily. The camels knew the way. Hundreds of years of Berber crossings had solidified the path beneath their leathery two-toed feet. They were as sure of it as the men who led them. Less sure were the traders and explorers who trailed behind the blue-robed men they had hired to carry them safely across the sand.

Most traders from the north were seeking the vast deposits of gold, iron, copper, and salt that coursed through the veins of sub-Saharan Africa. Just a century after Tin Hinan's founding of her city, gold dominated the African economy, providing work for thousands. People mined, melted, and purified the metal, chopped wood for the forges, created necessary tools, designed art, provided transport, and used their linguistic and diplomatic skill to make trades. Tales of rivers of gold beneath African soil sparked the imagination and glinted in greedy foreign eyes. Traders and explorers crossed the desert into the budding Empire of Ghana on the outskirts of the Sahara, near Africa's west coast, and returned with gold. They also returned with stories of gold-embroidered clothing, golden saddles, weapons mounted in gold, even dogs that wore gold or silver chains around their necks in this wealthy empire. The gold worked in West Africa, south of the Sahara, in land called the Bilad al-Sudan, or "Land of the Blacks," contributed to a global economy as well. In the fifth century, Europe was a tangle of warring tribes constantly migrating and fighting over land. There were the Celts, Angles, and Saxons of what would become the United Kingdom; the Franks of the future France; the Visigoths of what would soon be Portugal and Spain. The Vandals, Alani, Suebi, and Burgundian tribes crossed from east to west on the run from the Huns of central Asia, eventually making it as far as Spain. The Vandals continued on and eventually moved south into North Africa. Migration and war cost money. Europe's tribal leaders were so dependent on gold that without the trade routes that brought gold north, the European economy would have collapsed. Gold traveled north into the Sahara and was minted into coins. One North African mint at Sijilmasa coined gold, as did several Italian city-states. Gold made its way north and west, reaching all the way to Egypt, north across the Mediterranean to Spain and Rome, and into the Middle East. It wasn't only used for money. Art was covered in it. A majority of thirteenth-century Italian gold leaf used in paintings was made with West African gold.

Metallurgy supported empires and kingdoms from Egypt and Kush in the east, Ghana and Mali in the west, and as far south as the city of Great Zimbabwe. As a result, people became good at metal prospecting. They would scour the land for metal deposits to mine. Reading the landscape involved looking for a certain color in the soil that meant ore-bearing rocks or understanding rainfall cycles that would naturally separate metal deposits from the sand.

Each country had its own methods for finding gold. In

northern Zimbabwe, miners strapped weights to themselves to dive into the Mazowe and Rwenya Rivers to scoop sand from the bottom and take it to women and children on the surface, who would then separate out the gold. In Katanga, women worked alongside men in underground mines. But in some places, such as central African mines near modern-day Uganda, women were not allowed anywhere near the gold. Mining was cultural, and every culture had its own rules to follow.

An estimated five hundred to one thousand tons of gold passed through the Sahara annually at the peak of the trade route, from the fifth to eleventh centuries CE, not only from Ghana, but from other kingdoms with their own access to mines. However, gold wasn't all West Africa had to offer. As people dug beneath the ground, deposits of silver and iron had also been discovered, providing even more resources to trade. The Dogon of Mali's West African region smelted magnetite sand in down-draught furnaces to make both cast iron and soft iron. A South African mine in the Limpopo province was home to a copper mine that used twenty-five shafts dug into the ground to bring up the metal. Wood was used to keep the structure up, to make ladders, and as receptacles to carry the copper. One of these mines was so large that the miners carved around stone, leaving natural rock pillars in place as support.

The wealth of sub-Saharan Africa seemed to have no end. The people did not, however, give up their secrets. It was clear that trade hinged on their ability to maintain control of their natural resources. The Soninke people of Ghana kept the location of their mines a mystery. The Bambuk mines in partic-ular, located in what is now Mali and Senegal, were purposely shielded from Europeans, who marveled at just how much gold, iron, and silver there was pouring from south of the Sahara. Rumors were seeded along the trade routes that those who came in direct contact with the dark peoples from the Bilad al-Sudan were risking their very lives. Stories abounded of lethal snakes and beasts and the cannibalistic people who lived among them. Traders even went so far as to paint the miners as primal, saying that they bought the gold from people who were "naked."

Nothing could have been further from the truth. African empires and kingdoms built on gold had urban cities, systems of government, and established legal procedures. When the Europeans finally made it to the gold mines, they found farmers using everyday tools. No one went around naked. These fantastic stories were successful in keeping the curious away from the gold mines for a time, but they may have contributed to an idea about Africans that made it easier for Europeans to justify their enslavement years later.

In the mid 600s CE, a Muslim caliph by the name of Umar set his sights on leaving Saudi Arabia in order to spread Islam, then limited to the Arabian Peninsula, across the world. His army traveled north to conquer Persia. Then Umar turned his sights south, infiltrating Africa, increasing his army with converts from traditional animist religions and having them bring their newly learned Muslim religion as they marched on. He was killed by a Christian slave named Abu Lu'lu'ah, and his successor, Uthman ibn Affan, continued the Muslim expansion. When Affan died, yet another caliph took over to further their conquest.

The Muslims conquered what was once Berber land, capturing Carthage in 698 and Tangiers in 708. Then they made their way down the profitable trade routes. They conquered and converted as they went. The Berbers, accustomed as they were to adaptation, shifted from their indigenous, animist religions to Islam. Arabic words were added to their native Amazigh languages, such as the soft and soulful Tamazight, Kabyle, and Tamahaq.

Next, the Arabs moved south and east into the Kingdom of Axum, which had taken over Kushite and Ethiopian lands centuries before, and destroyed the key trading port city of Adulis in 710. With other strategic trading points in their possession, the Arabs influenced trading practices and brought standard weights and measures to bargaining procedures. Every trader was responsible for making and carrying his own weights to measure the goods he was buying—and to ensure he got the best deal. The Arab weights were simple shapes. If they had designs on the surfaces, they were abstract or geometric. But Africans, who had a centuries-old tradition of making artistry part of everyday life, elevated the mundane objects to new creative heights, crafting weights that were as beautiful as they were practical. They cast brass figures that expressed the proverbs and philosophies of the region and the time.

Every part of the process of dealing with metals across the African continent was both scientific and cultural. In African hands every weight was a piece of art, a work of literature, and a lesson in philosophy that reflected the personal values of the trader who carried it. In noisy markets, parched, dusty traders wound through crowds with their loud, spitting, smelly camels, looking for just the right deal. And when they found a bargain, they pulled weights that shone in the sunlight out of their packs. The intricate, elegant, and mathematically precise pieces were often as precious as the goods that were being haggled over, and they put the beauty and artistry of African peoples on full display to foreign traders.

Trusting in wealth is like looking
for feathers on turtles.

MANSA MUSA: THE RICHEST MAN OF ALL TIME

{Muhn-sah Moo-sah}

Musa was never supposed to be the mansa, or emperor, of Mali. He was of royal blood, but the line of succession was to go through his elder brother, Abubakari II, and skip him entirely. So his boyhood wasn't burdened with the worries of what it meant to be a leader. He knew he would have a good position because of his family. He might be the governor of some region, answering to his elder brother, but ruling was not his destiny. Until it was.

Musa's grandfather was Sundiata Keita. Keita organized some of the peoples who had fractured from the dying Empire of Ghana in the early 1200s CE. Like all the empires and kingdoms before it, Ghana's did not last forever. By the thirteenth century it was in decline, and Sundiata Keita was one of several kings in the region who warred with one another over control of the land. Two main groups formed: the Susu and the Malinke. Sundiata Keita ruled over the Malinke people.

In 1235 CE, Sundiata Keita's armies took on the Susu and absorbed their lands. Next he worked on expanding the borders of his people. By the time Keita was finished, the new empire, Mali, stretched from the Atlantic Coast all the way to the city of Gao on the bend of the Niger River. Keita became the first of the mansas, or emperors, of Mali.

Keita worked to establish a system of government and rule of law that would keep the empire standing long after he was gone. Provinces were set up, each with a governor, and each town within the province had a mayor or mochrif. The government was hierarchical, with men of lesser power answering to men of greater power, all the way up to the mansa himself. After Keita's death, rule passed to his sons and eventually to his grandson, Abubakari II.

Like his grandfather before him, Abubakari II was interested in expanding Mali's borders, but the new mansa took this mission to an extreme. Expansion along the lands around Mali was not enough. Abubakari II turned his attention to the western border of his empire, where the Atlantic Ocean lay. He wanted to cross the ocean to conquer the unseen lands that he knew must be on the other side.

Abubakari II gathered his sailors on Mali's western shore and ordered them to sail into uncharted waters until they had found land or their food and supplies had run short. The men set out with only the assurance of their mansa that they would find dry land somewhere beyond the thin blue horizon.

On the sea, one ship lagged behind, and as it did, its sailors saw a broad current overtake the ships ahead and sweep them up and under the ocean. Suddenly, they were the only ship left. The captain ordered the boat to be turned around, and they headed back for Mali to avoid the same fate as the rest of the fleet.

The loss of his ships and his men didn't stop Mansa Abubakari II from trying again. The mansa decided to make a second expedition. This time, he ordered a much larger fleet of two thousand pirogues, boats often made from carving out a single log, and to ensure this expedition's success, he decided that he would command it himself. The journey was uncertain, and Abubakari II had no idea when he would return—if ever—which would leave the empire vulnerable. He was willing to risk his own life for the sake of exploration and discovery, but he would not risk his country, so he decided to give up his throne. He called for his brother, Musa, to step in.

While Abubakari II was on his expedition, Musa would rule as mansa of Mali. If Abubakari II did not return in a reasonable amount of time, Musa would inherit the throne permanently. With the matter of the empire's leadership taken care of, Abubakari II's second fleet set sail in 1311 from the coast of present-day Gambia, headed for a shore they couldn't see, knowing that they might never set foot on their own again.

Abubakari II never returned to Mali. Mansa Musa came into full power in 1312, one year after his brother had set out.

There was little opposition to the vast empire that dominated this area of West Africa, so Musa focused on expanding Mali's borders—on land. Musa's army moved southward, taking control of several gold mines that lay outside their borders, and north, taking over a salt mine along one of the crucial trade routes. By the end of his rule, he had added about twenty-four more cities to the empire. On a modern map, Mansa Musa's empire would stretch across nine countries, some 430,000 square miles. Five trade routes now came through his borders, and he controlled them all, squeezing out any traders but those under his reign and taxing merchants going in and coming out of the empire. He also reconquered parts of the kingdom that had slipped away during the reign of less able mansas and demanded tributes and gifts from their rulers.

Mansa Musa ruled over forty million people, yet there was peace during his twenty-five-year reign, likely because Musa was smart about how to use the royal coffers. He donated money to people and built schools and mosques. Because Musa levied taxes against merchants as they came and went, the Malian people themselves did not have to pay taxes. It was a smart move that ensured peace inside the country. There was peace on the borders, too. No one wanted to take on a behemoth like Mali. But peace from internal and external conflict didn't mean that the people of the empire didn't occasionally have disputes with one another. To settle them, they would have to see the mansa himself.

Like all previous mansas, Musa held court in his palace. These royal audiences with his subjects were the only place where grievances could be heard and answered. On court days, horns and drums alerted people that the proceedings were about to begin. Thick crowds flocked to a tree-lined street facing an alcove that led into the palace, in which the mansa was seated. The alcove had two stories, with three silver-foiled window frames on the second floor and three on the first floor plated in gold. Curtains covered in Egyptian designs rustled in the wind, each tied back by silk cord from faraway China.

Once the horns and drums had summoned everyone, the parade began. Three hundred soldiers marched in two deep and stood on either side of the alcove. In the first row, archers sat with their bows, and in the second row, soldiers stood behind them holding their javelins. Two horses and two rams were brought up to await their ceremonial use. Then came people necessary to the proceedings: preachers and jurists (law experts) took their seats around the soldiers. A herald, or griot (also sometimes called a jeli), stood at the entrance, resplendent in a large, fluffy turban with a gold scabbard for his sword, wearing boot spurs and holding gold and silver javelins with iron tips. He ensured that only those who were part of the mansa's audience were on the inside of the alcove.

Next, dignitaries arrived, each one preceded by the music of elephant-tusk horns and drums and each one carrying blades and bows. They came with their own entourages, which went ahead of them either on foot or on horseback.

After everyone had settled, the mansa himself made his way to the alcove, preceded by singers walking slowly and carrying gold and silver vessels. The mansa carried a gold bow and had a golden quiver at his back. He wore a gold turban with ribbons that ended in metal tips about the length of a hand. He wore a red coat made of European cloth. Behind him, another three hundred soldiers followed. When the mansa took his throne, the horns, trumpets, and drums sounded again. Now the horses and rams that had been let in earlier did their duty. They made their way back through the crowd, driving out bad luck.

Only then did the griot, the one person at court assigned to speak for and to the mansa, begin the proceedings. A person with a grievance would enter the alcove, first taking off their hat and shoes as a sign of respect to the mansa. They would also throw dust on their head in a show of reverence and bow low. The person would tell the griot their grievances, which the griot would then repeat to the mansa. The mansa then whispered his opinion to the griot, who repeated it to everyone at court in a ringing voice, often in song.

It would have been a breathtaking scene—precise, controlled, and dripping with ritual.

‡

Under Musa's rule, Mali's borders expanded. The empire's wealth grew daily. Peace reigned. So now Musa turned inward, interested in improving not the empire, but himself.

Mansa Musa was a Muslim. All Muslims who are able are required, by religious law, to take the hajj, a pilgrimage to the holy land, Mecca, in Saudi Arabia. For Musa it was a journey of about four thousand miles through several countries, over the treacherous terrain of the Sahara, and then across the Red Sea. It would be an enormous undertaking. His advisers told him to plan for an ambitious trek, and plan he did. In 1324, he embarked on what was probably a journey of unprecedented scale. Not only would Mansa Musa tackle the four-thousand-mile hike east through the widest part of Africa and then across the Red Sea to Saudi Arabia—he would do it with an entourage of sixty thousand people, including twelve thousand servants. His senior wife (he had several) went along on the journey, bringing with her five hundred personal maids. They took with them supplies for the journey: tents, bedding, clothes, food, water, gifts, and, of course, gold. Eighty camels were loaded with about three hundred pounds of gold each, and the people Mansa Musa enslaved carried another twenty-four tons of it.

Mansa Musa traveled in style. Five hundred heralds, wearing Persian silk and carrying four-foot-long golden staffs that glistened blindingly in the sun, led the entire entourage. Following them were armed royal guards, some carrying spears, others carrying swords, and some bearing the flags of the empire. They wore gold bracelets, necklaces, and anklets. Musa's horse was outfitted in gold, and it's likely that Musa himself would have brought his golden arms.

Musa and his entourage began their pilgrimage at one of the many Saharan trade routes within Mali's borders. They set off, a massive line of people stretching along the sand for as far as the eye could see, bringing with them Musa's incredible wealth on full display. Musa gave freely from the wealth he carried, stunning people from small states and larger kingdoms all the way to the Red Sea, including the people who worked in the Takedda mines, east of Mali's borders, and the citizens of the central African kingdom of Kanem-Bornu in the Lake Chad region. He passed out gold not only to dignitaries and kings that he met but to ordinary people, the poor, the ill and infirm, anyone he deemed needed it. On Fridays, wherever they set up their tents for the night, Musa ordered a mosque to be built in that location.

Word of Mansa Musa's generosity preceded him. Soon, wherever they went, Musa's entourage was enthusiastically welcomed and well looked after. By the time they reached the city of Cairo in Egypt, Egyptian merchants, thrilled at the prospect of a wealthy emperor in their midst, prepared to take full advantage. They charged exorbitant prices for their wares, which Musa easily paid.

Mansa Musa stayed in Cairo three months, long enough for the local merchants to have their fill and the local peoples to benefit from his seemingly boundless generosity. But while he caused a sensation in the markets, he also spent the time there working to make diplomatic contacts. He met with the sultan and opened up trading routes from that corner of North Africa all the way across to Musa's empire in the west. Musa then sailed across the Red Sea to Mecca to complete the hajj.

With his religious obligations fulfilled, Musa returned to Mali a year later, significantly poorer in gold, but with new avenues of trade for Mali and goodwill in countries all over the north of the continent. His fame grew far and wide. Stories about his epic journey mesmerized people not just in Africa, but throughout Europe and Asia.

The mansa picked up a few people on his way back to Mali. One of them, an architect and poet from Andalusia named Abu

Ishaz al-Sahili, came back with the mansa specifically to erect buildings in Mali. Under this architect's influence, domed palaces became the norm, replacing some of the more geometric, straight-edged constructions that had existed before. Mansa Musa ordered a great mosque to be built at Timbuktu, and a few years later, he ordered another at Sankore. After the mosques' construction, both cities and the surrounding areas became centers of learning that people flocked to from all over the world. By 1450, long after Musa was gone, there were a reported one hundred thousand people living in Timbuktu. Twenty-five thousand of them were students, mainly from African countries, but some were from Europe and the Middle East.

At his wealthiest, Mansa Musa was worth about four hundred billion dollars by today's standards, making him the richest person in world history. His wealth and fame were so widespread that it literally put him and Mali on the map. An image of him was included in the Catalan Atlas, a map of the medieval world created in 1375 by mapmaker Abraham Cresques. It was commissioned by a European king forty years after Mansa Musa's death.

THE CATALAN ATLAS

As storied as he was in his own lifetime and beyond, there is only one known existing depiction of Mansa Musa. It appears in the Catalan Atlas. The mapmaker, Abraham Cresques, came from a long line of mapmakers in Majorca, Spain, who gathered accounts from sailors, diplomats, and traders (including the famed Marco Polo) to gain as precise a perspective of land and water routes, political makeups, and natural resources around the globe as they could. As the mapmaker to King Pedro IV of Aragon, Cresques was renowned for his work. The Catalan map was meant to be a gift to King Charles V of France commissioned by Pedro as a gift of diplomacy. Maps from Catalan were part of the goods Pedro traded, because they were considered to be the best in the world at the time and would have made an impressive gift. It is made up of six heavily illustrated panels that feature important figures as well as the known world's geography. In one panel, Mansa Musa is shown holding a large golden orb and a gold scepter as he is approached by another figure on camelback.

The Catalan Atlas was meant to be viewed in the round, so whatever side you were viewing the map from, the images on the opposite side are upside down. It was also meant to

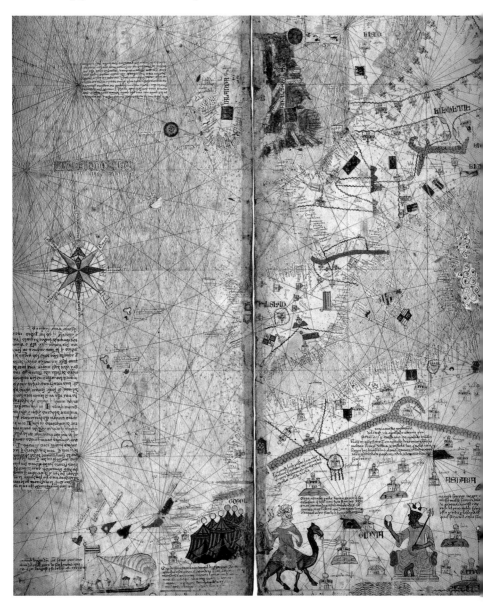

be viewed with the south at the top and the north below. The way it mostly appears in books is exactly the opposite of what Cresques had intended, but in keeping with the way we use maps today, with the south at the bottom edge and the north on top.

THE POWER OF
THE GRIOT

The griot, or jeli, a kind of combination storyteller, poet, and musician, was vital to communication in royal court. In the Malian tradition, mansas were not to speak above a whisper, so their wishes had to be conveyed by others. They also could not be spoken to directly, which made a go-between necessary. In West Africa (as in some other parts of the continent) it was believed that a person's talent and skill were a god-given gift that a person could only be born into. Work followed family lines: weavers, miners, farmers, and even the griots followed matrilineal lines, with skills passing from men to their nephews.

The griots were trained in history, poetry, oratory, and music. Their role was to give living accounts of history, to sing songs that praised rulers and encouraged the fearful in times of war. Griots memorized all the stories of their people. When a griot neared the end of his life, he would teach the next generation all the stories so they would never be forgotten. Griots were at court during the hearing of cases, embellishing and fine-tuning the complaints of the people for the king's benefit and relaying the king's verdicts in the most beautiful manner. They went into war, not to fight but to encourage those on the battlefield and inspire them to acts of supreme bravery even in the face of death.

Griots continually lauded the ruling class and reminded everyone else of their storied history. Their songs of praise were accompanied by the bala (or balafon), a kind of xylophone that they played. There were sometimes entire choruses of jeli behind the main griot, wearing birdlike masks and singing praise songs themselves.

The praise songs of the griot could be very influential, even to royalty. Otsman, Mansa Musa's brother, having been lectured by his mother to not steal the throne away from Musa when Abubakari II failed to return, set off to pay his brother homage the year Musa took the throne permanently. He moved ahead of his troops, his griot at his side. The praise song of the griot about Otsman's deeds moved Otsman to such pride that he stopped his journey. He decided he would not bow to his brother, regardless of his status as mansa. Instead, he turned to his men and ordered them to unload the food he was taking to Mansa Musa as tribute. "Unload everything on the boats," he said. "Upon my life, the one speaking to you will no longer put any dust on his head for anyone."

LIBRARIES IN THE SAND

Timbuktu, located in the junction between the dry Sahara and the lush Niger valley, was the perfect place for caravans to stop and rest. Most believe the city was founded in the eleventh century by a Tuareg woman named Bouctou who managed a rest stop for camel caravans on the Niger River. ("Tin Bouctou" means "the well of Bouctou.") For centuries, people broke from their dusty journeys to cool themselves in the city. Camels exhausted from their long treks were left to pasture and drink. And every traveler, merchant, guide, and hired guard relished the opportunity to get a well-earned rest before continuing on. Before long, Timbuktu became more than a temporary stop and grew into a rich and cultured city.

By the mid-sixteenth century it was a crossroads of trade. Caravans from the desert and boats from the river brought traders and goods. Wood, gold, salt, glass beads, ceramics, and ivory made their way through the city; local and foreign cloth was sold in bazaars; the air was scented with spices, food, oil, peppers, and perfumes, and artisans worked, making cloth, jewelry, and even drawing designs on women's skin with an ink made from the abundant henna trees in the region. For these goods and services, gold nuggets and cowrie shells were the main currency. For the one hundred thousand people who lived in Timbuktu, it was not only a trading center but a center of religion and education, thanks in part to the mosques and schools Mansa Musa insisted on building there.

The city housed huge libraries filled with books that covered every subject imaginable. There were books on astronomy, medicine, law, theology, grammar, and proverbs. Other books included dictionaries, diaries, letters from rulers, legal opinions, historical texts, and works of poetry—all of them carefully handwritten.

Books were big business and were part of the regular trans-Saharan trade. They came by caravan from northern cities such as Fez, Cairo, Tripoli, and Cordoba, to be sold to scholars in the markets of Timbuktu. Sometimes scholars themselves traveled to faraway cities, like Cairo, in order to copy books there and then bring the copies back home. Many other manuscripts were painstakingly hand-copied in Timbuktu itself. Some of these manuscripts were so old, their pages were in hazard of turning to dust, and the only way to preserve them was to copy them afresh. In room after room, by sunlight, lamplight, and moonlight, were the dark bodies of the most learned men, who hunched over delicate paper made of linen and fish skin, painstakingly rewriting texts in gorgeous, precise script, with ink and dyes made from desert plants, and then bound the pages in sheep or goat leather. The pages were covered not only in traditional Arabic calligraphy but also in designs, illustrations, and geometric shapes. Even corrections to mistakes penned carefully into the margins looked like works of art.

When Mansa Musa was in power, he oversaw the establishment of several madrassas in the area, schools where young people could learn the teachings of the Qur'an, the holy book of Islam. There was a full curriculum of learning that the students could embark on if they chose to become scholars. The most learned scholars spent decades on their schooling, following an intensive curriculum of subjects, including botany, theology, Islamic law, grammar, rhetoric, logic, history, geography, astronomy, astrology, mathematics (including calculus and geometry), music, medicine, and surgery. Students were expected to write down texts read to them by their teachers, sometimes in the teacher's home so students would have access to their teacher's own extensive libraries. At the end of a period of study, professors would write out diplomas to give to their pupils. Their education was enviable. One of the people Musa brought back from his hajj, a scholar named Abderrahman-El-Temini, was invited to Mali for his knowledge of the law. However, when he arrived, he discovered that the local Sudanese legal experts in Timbuktu knew much more than he did. Rather than starting work as a teacher there as he had expected to do, he became a student himself.

A century after Mansa Musa's rule, when the Empire of Mali fell to the nearby Songhai Empire, scholarship grew to be more than the mere emulation of already established works. Rather than simply copying the words of others, scholars began writing their own texts. The city's famed book trade continued to grow. By 1510, when Leo Africanus, a sixteen-year-old student and explorer from the Moroccan city of Fez, traveled south to Timbuktu, he reported on the value of manuscripts there. "There is more profit made from this commerce than from all other merchandise." He described the town as a vibrant intellectual community "full of Sudanese students, Westerners, in ardent pursuit of science and virtue."

Initially, the manuscripts copied by scribes in Timbuktu were purchased or commissioned for personal libraries. The homes of the most elite in society were filled with them. One of Timbuktu's most celebrated scholars, Ahmed Baba (1556–1627), who liked to be called Ahmed Baba the Black, said that his personal library of 1,600 manuscripts was one of the smaller collections in the city. His legal opinions (called "fatwas") were noted for their clarity and attention to Islamic principles. His biographical dictionary covering jurists (lawyers) and Moroccan religious personalities remains an important source for historians.

The opinions of Baba and his colleagues covered a range of topics. There were agreements about how to use gold as a standard value. A document was drawn up to give a woman her freedom from her enslaver. Laws addressed under what circumstances a person could become enslaved and then regain their freedom. There were arguments in favor of peace, an argument against the jailing of a German man who made his way to a restricted place, rules for ethical behavior, advice, and information about diseases and their cures.

Askia Daoud ("askia" is the word for "king" among the Songhai) established public libraries during his reign from 1548 to 1583, expanding the reach of the written word to those who might not have been able to afford the high price of literature. He also employed scribes to copy manuscripts and gave these as presents. One of the items he gave as a gift was the Qamus dictionary, which was valued at eighty mithqal. Each mithqal was equal to 4.25 grams of gold, giving the dictionary a value of nearly $17,000 by today's standards.

Sadly, these libraries would not survive. Moroccan forces seized Timbuktu in 1593. In the wake of their victory, they killed, captured, or exiled the city's elite, including jurists, scribes, and scholars like Ahmed Baba. They also destroyed buildings, including all the public libraries. The destruction of the great city and decimation of the people were insurmountable. Timbuktu suffered for centuries, its scholars gone, its people scattered, its storied history ground into the dirt. What was left of the beautiful books and handwritten opinions among Timbuktu's survivors was squirreled away in lockboxes, hidden in homes, and fiercely guarded. In the late nineteenth century, when the French occupied Mali, fear for the surviving literature again rose to a quiver. Like the Moroccans, the French destroyed what they came across, and it fell once again to the people of Timbuktu to protect their delicate legacy. False walls were built into homes to hide laden bookshelves. Manuscripts were sealed in boxes and placed under floors. Some were buried directly under the Sahara sand. Many of them would never be seen again.

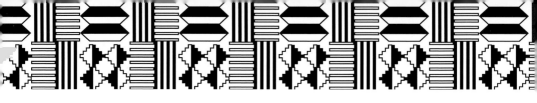

THE WINDS CHANGE

At the close of the fifteenth century, major changes were on the horizon for the people of Africa, especially along the western shore. Mansa Musa's famed leadership was long gone, and the power of Mali had faded. Another kingdom rose in the same location in what is now present-day Nigeria: the Kingdom of Benin. This kingdom benefitted from the natural resources of its vast forests fed by the Niger River. They traded via the trans-Saharan route in palm oil, pepper, and ivory to build their wealth and stability. But this route was losing its influence. For many years, Europeans had been trying to find a way to avoid the long and arduous trek. Sailing south down the west coast of Africa seemed a promising possibility, but the Atlantic Ocean was tricky, different from the Mediterranean that they understood so well. Little did they know it was the Sahara itself that kept them back, even on the sea. Hot desert winds blew west across the water, preventing European vessels from returning after a certain point. Finally, at the end of the fifteenth century, the Portuguese made two discoveries that gave them a way to go farther along the African coast. First was the caravel, a light ship with three masts that made it possible for the sails to handle unfavorable winds. Second was a new sailing technique called the "volta do mar lago," where sailors turned their ship against the wind on the open sea.

Now merchandise could flow across the water between Africa and Europe much faster and with less danger than taking it across the Sahara. Going over the sea was also cheaper. It meant fewer payouts to guides and armed guards for protection inside the desert and fewer taxes paid in tribute to African kings every time a merchant crossed into their lands.

The African kings turned their heads from the inland trade routes and toward the sea, watching the coasts carefully to protect them from raiding European ships. The Portuguese were the first to invade the West African coast, making their way into lands dominated by Mandé-speaking people, including what would become the countries of Sierra Leone, Senegal, and Ghana. They sailed farther south and allied themselves with the king of the Kongo. Eventually the Portuguese circumnavigated the continent and colonized Mozambique.

The Portuguese had decades to establish themselves, but eventually, other European nations made their way to the continent. The French colonized the north and west, taking land that belonged to the Berbers and Tuareg people. This would become the countries of Morocco and Algeria, among others. Britain took land in the south that belonged to the Bantu ethnic group, as well as eastern lands, imposing themselves on the entire length of the continent.

The many Europeans who came over the water weren't

interested in peaceful trade, as they had been when they relied on African guides, translators, and diplomacy to trade within the continent. On their own ships, they were looking to enslave people and to extract natural resources that they could use to make money without the authority of any king but their own in Europe. So many African people had been forcibly taken to Europe that residents were alarmed. By the early sixteenth century, about ten percent of the population of the Portuguese capital, Lisbon, were enslaved Africans. In England, Elizabeth I complained that "Negroes and black Moors" should be expelled from London over concern about their numbers.

In the Kingdom of Benin, the formidable Queen Idia was paying attention. She wanted to ensure that her son would have the best chance at dealing with the winds of change that were coming from Europe. And while her boy was not the only son in line for the throne, she intended to give him his best chance.

QUEEN IDIA: KINGMAKER

{Ih-dee-uh}

Queen Idia was married to Ozolua, the oba (king) of Benin. Her husband was strong and capable, and he ruled over the rising Kingdom of Benin. She ruled at his side, riding with him into battle, advising him, and using her knowledge of medicine and the mystical arts (speaking with the ancestors, divining the future, and reading signs in nature) to help him make the kingdom strong. But all the while, she looked to her son Esigie and prepared him for the task of leadership. She used the opportunity of the Portuguese interest in peaceful trade to make sure her son could speak fluent Portuguese and deal with these men without a translator.

When Oba Ozolua died in 1504, Esigie was not the only son who could inherit the throne. He had a brother, Arhuaran, also a powerful prince, and both of them wanted to be the next oba. The sons controlled two important cities in the kingdom. Esigie held power in Benin City, and Arhuaran held power in the city of Udo. With the brothers' eyes set on the throne, the country was immediately plunged into a civil war. Ozolu's two sons amassed their armies and attacked each other in a furious bid to gain control of the country.

Neighboring countries were thrilled. With Benin fighting a civil war, it was a perfect opportunity to topple the mighty kingdom, or at least weaken it enough so that those countries on the borders could benefit. The Igala people occupied the left (eastern) bank of the Niger River in a small kingdom on Benin's border. They had risen to power in the 1400s alongside the fledgling Kingdom of Benin and two other empires, the Nupe and the Oyo, but they did not grow to the massive force that Benin did. However, even a small force might be able to take on a country whose military might was focused on an internal war.

Sensing their opportunity, the Igala sent warriors across the Benue River.

Esigie was busy fighting his brother, but Idia was ready. She put together an army to help Esigie and took up the role of Esigie's military strategist. With Idia's army on his side, Esigie's advances against his brother were successful. Arhuaran's forces were pushed back, and Esigie finally controlled the country. Then Esigie's forces turned their attention to the invading Igala and, again with Idia's help, stopped their attacks. When the fighting ended, Idia knew enough about medicine to help heal the wounded.

Without resistance from invaders outside the kingdom, or within it from his own brother, Esigie was able to take the throne and become oba. To thank his mother for her help, he created a new court position called the "iyoba," or queen mother. It gave Idia political power on the same level as that of senior town chiefs, who, along with the palace chiefs, were responsible for the administration of the kingdom. She was also given a specially built court residence of her own called the Eguae-Iyoba (Palace of the Queen Mother), along with a staff of her own. Queen mothers in Benin had always held influence, but they had not had an official title or residence prior to Idia's rule.

Esigie ordered court artists to create the likeness of his mother. They carved her face in ivory, cast it in bronze, and etched it in wood. Each one captured her strong, slender face and piercing eyes, but these were no mere portraits. Their sculptures made a statement about all Idia meant to the Oba and to the people of Benin. It was at once a way to honor the woman who wielded so much influence on the kingdom and to show her contribution to its culture.

What the court artists created was a new style of portraiture that would become famous in Benin. The pieces were highly detailed, and their work mirrored reality so closely that Europeans thought the Benin bronze faces had been cast on the faces of the dead. They weren't, of course. What artisans used was a centuries-old lost-wax method of casting bronze, a method by which a skillfully carved wax model is melted away (or "lost") and molten bronze is poured into the space left behind.

One of the most famous of Esigie's commissioned art pieces was a carving of Idia crafted by the executive guild of royal ivory carvers, a large pendant meant to be worn at the hip by the oba himself.

In the carving, the Queen Mother's elegant face is detailed in ivory. White was the symbol of ancestry and also represented the reflective nature of water. So a piece of white art made a connection to the ancestors, who were believed to go across the water at their death. Idia's head is framed with a crown, with two rows of short braids plaited behind it. The crown itself shows Portuguese men with mustaches wearing hats. Mustaches—and any kind of facial hair—were something of a curiosity to the people of West Africa. Most men, certainly the ones who lived in Benin, did not grow out their facial hair. Nonetheless, these mustached men were thought to have a certain mystical quality. They had, after all, arrived on the water, had white skin, and had the same kind of mustaches that the mudfish, native to rivers in Benin, another symbol of mystical power, wore. The Portuguese also brought with them money and trading opportunities. The inclusion of the Portuguese in the pendant would likely have spoken volumes about the trading opportunities that Esigie, fluent in Portuguese, would keep open for the kingdom.

Between the Portuguese men on Idia's carved portrait are mudfish. The mudfish lives both on land and in the water and was a powerful symbol of people who could influence both the real world and the world of the ancestors. Idia was considered to have mystical powers, so it's no wonder the mudfish is used in her portrait. Wrapped under her neck is a collar of coral beads, another nod to water, which is where coral is found, and beneath that is an openwork collar of more Portuguese heads.

On Idia's forehead, over her eyes, are two metal strips of iron and copper. Their reflective surfaces also symbolize water. Additionally, the metals in the portrait were meant to show Queen Mother Idia's strength. Their location on her face, above her eyes, is another nod to her mystical knowledge and her ability to take and give advice from the ancestors.

The graceful, detailed piece is masterly in its delicate treatment of Queen Mother Idia's face, but also in the scope of its representation of the belief system of the Kingdom of Benin.

Idia oversaw the successful transition of power from her husband to her son and ensured his successful diplomatic ties with Portugal—a first for the kingdom. And she ensured power for future iyobas, another first for a kingdom that had been patriarchal to its core. Thanks to Idia, all future iyobas were important because of their connection to their sons, so much so that after an iyoba had her first son, she wouldn't even try to have any more children. Instead, she would devote her life to raising and training her young prince for his eventual position as oba. In this way, Idia made iyobas vital to the protection and continuation of the line of obas.

Sadly, Idia's influence and protection would not extend far into the future. The Kingdom of Benin collapsed in the late nineteenth century, and Idia's portraits were looted by the British. Today there are two known ivory sculpture pendants of Idia. One of them is in the Metropolitan Museum of Art in New York City. The other is in the British Museum. Neither has been given back to Nigeria, despite the Nigerian government's requests for their return.

CULTURE LOST

A hundred years after Esigie's rule, in the middle of the seventeenth century, the trade relationships between African nations and the European countries built mostly on African gold were disintegrating. Once the Portuguese found a way to navigate ships down the west coast of Africa, the Saharan routes were used less and less. The African guides, guards, and merchants who relied on the overland crossings for their livelihood found the demand for their skills shrinking. The Portuguese—and on their heels, France, Spain, and England—now had fast, direct access to African kingdoms. And while trade between Africa and Europe continued up to the nineteenth century, Europe was looking for a way to circumvent peaceful enterprise. They found it in guns, which they had and the African nations did not. With guns, the Europeans did not need to bow low in the crowded courts of African kings. They did not have to speak only to the kings' griots and throw dust on their own heads as a sign of respect. These Europeans could take what they wanted by force. And what they wanted were African resources, including its people.

The largest forced enslavement of human beings in the

history of the world had begun. Europe's nations colonized African lands, settling on them as if they were their own. One after another African kingdom fell. African culture was forcibly eliminated at the point of a gun in favor of European customs, style of dress, and religion. With the forcible removal of people, including the griots and jeli who held the history of their lands on their tongues, Africa lost its connection to the past, its culture, its beliefs, and sometimes even its languages. The manuscripts in centers of learning in Timbuktu were hidden away from the invading French. By the time they were recovered and brought out into fresh air more than a century later, many of the pages turned to dust in the eager hands of the descendants who were to have inherited them. Some were victims of rot. Many others had been destroyed by insects, the delicate paper and weighty words passing through the digestive tracts of small creatures, never to be read again. With the griots rounded up and shipped to foreign lands along with doctors, philosophers, artisans, jurists, royalty, architects, farmers, and more, and the stories that told the history of Africa hidden away in fear, what eventually took its place was European history, as if Africans had never had their own.

All across the continent, African people resisted colonization in an attempt to hold on to their culture, their history, their lands, and their people. But resistance against European guns was mostly futile. Ethiopia was the only country that successfully resisted European rule. However, its emperor, Tewodros II, took his own life rather than fall to the British. As he lay dead on the ground, the locks of his hair were cut off and taken as a prize. Worse, his seven-year-old son, Prince Alemayehu, was taken by British forces to England. The prince never saw his homeland again. While his father's hair was eventually returned, the prince's bones remain in Windsor Palace, despite requests by the Ethiopian government for their return.

Still, the many histories of the African people and their countries could not be erased entirely. The sheer innovation, artistry, skill, and scholarship of the continent's peoples live on despite every attempt to quench them. African art created over centuries survives as artifacts that made it across the Sahara to foreign countries. Ivory sculptures created for customers in Europe can be found in museums around the world. Long-buried artifacts found in archaeological digs have revealed that the people of Zaire had their own number system.

The Yoruba of Nigeria had a math system based on units of 20 (modern math uses a base 10 system). Egyptians charted the movement of the sun and stars and divided the year into 12 seg-ments. A structure built in modern-day Kenya in 300 BCE called "African Stonehenge" was used as a calendar. The Dogon of Mali had a deep understanding of astronomy. They knew that Saturn had rings, that there were moons around Jupiter, that the star Sirius B existed—thousands of years before there was a telescope to prove it—and they plotted orbits in our solar system up to the year 1990.

Recent archaeological discoveries are giving us more information about Africa. A 2019 dig found workshops in Egypt's Valley of the Kings dating back three thousand years that were dedicated to firing and painting pottery, making furniture, and cleaning gold. They have also revealed that workers wrote poetry on some of that pottery. Also in 2019, thirty coffins were found near Luxor, Egypt, with perfectly preserved mummies inside. The 4,400-year-old tomb of an official named Kuwy was also discovered, revealing paintings that still showed vibrant color, the way they might have been when they were first painted. These are just a few examples, and all focus on one area of the continent. Discoveries across the rest of the continent are still waiting.

That African peoples had connections to people in Europe and Asia is also hard to ignore. The metalwork of people in the region that is now Rwanda, Tanzania, and Uganda surpassed that of Europeans of 1,500 to 2,000 years ago, so much so that Europeans imported their tools and weapons from Africa. African gold is leafed on Italian paintings. African ivory was carved and sent to Europe. Bronze bowls from European kings made their way to sub-Saharan countries. Glass beads from Venice cover sculptures made by the people of Lake Chad. These objects tell the story of peoples who were deeply connected to others around the globe, who freely exchanged their cultures, who relied on one another in one way or another . . . at least for a while.

What remains is a fractured history of a diverse and astounding continent that is still being pieced together. So much of it is missing, but scholars continue to study Africa, finding more details about the people and their innovations, art, and customs, once prevalent and influential around the globe.

AUTHOR'S NOTE

From the ancient times of the very first populations that moved up and out of the continent from the southernmost regions of Africa, taking ideas and innovations with them, Africa has fueled the world. The wealth of Africa sustained economies during the Middle Ages via the trans-Saharan trade routes, and then later, when transatlantic trade began, people taken from their homes and enslaved built the economies of the Americas and Europe. Riches are still being extracted from Africa at an alarming rate. The north of Africa is full of petroleum and gas. Iron ore is still extracted from the northwest. Vast deposits of gold are being mined in the same regions that were once the lands of Mansa Musa and Queen Idia of Esigie, as well as in the areas that once were the kingdoms of the kandakes and Ethiopia. The land from central to southern Africa is flush with diamonds. Platinum is also found in the southwest. Natural resources from across the continent valued at $203 billion annually enrich the rest of the world, but the people of Africa don't have access to them because of the way European countries and businesses have carved up the continent and access to it.

There is still so much to say about the history of Africa. I've barely scratched the surface here. So many stories of people and places haven't been touched in this book, and there are many more that are yet to be discovered. Fascinating stories that didn't fit into this volume include the story of Mwana Mkisi, the female founder of Mombassa. I wish I could have found out more about her, but there is barely a mention in the historical record. What I found was this: *Gongwa nda Mwana Mkisi, Mvita mji wa kale Usitupile viasi, ukenda enda kwa.* This means: *Gongwa is the royal land of Mwana Mkisi, Mvita is a city of old. Do not exceed the bounds, but tread warily therein.* Who was this amazing woman?

I also wanted to talk about the Nok peoples of Nigeria and the incredible artworks they developed before the common era. Their style and firing techniques certainly influenced the development of African art, and it's possible to trace the high artistry of the Benin Bronzes all the way back to this ancestral art form.

Bouctou, the female founder of Timbuktu, and the scholar Ahmed Baba the Black also deserve much more attention than I have given them here. Then there is the Dogon of Mali, whose ancient religion somehow incorporated the existence of the star Sirius B long before modern scientists had even conceived of it or eventually saw it in super-powerful telescopes. I hope the stories I was able to tell in this book will serve as a beginning. Every day we learn more about Africa. Every day, another piece of the puzzle that tells the diverse stories of African culture falls into place, helping to complete the picture. Still, so much more needs to be discovered and written down. Africa is civilization's oldest home, the holder of the world's longest and most lasting history, yet we still know so little of its whole truth. With your help, we can discover even more and see that it will not be lost forever. Perhaps we can give something back to the mighty continent from which so much has been taken.

ACKNOWLEDGMENTS

This book would not have been possible without the help of several people, including experts in the field of African studies who were generous in answering questions, reading and commenting on sections, and directing me to further sources. My thanks go to Elise Howard, for suggesting the book in the first place; Martha Brockenbrough, for helping with an entry-point to research; Chris Lynch, for allowing me to talk through ideas; Dr. Yaëlle Biro, for the personal tour at the Metropolitan Museum of Art; Rachel Dwyer at the African Studies Library at Boston University; Bassey Irele, Librarian for Sub-Saharan Africa at Harvard University; Bettiann McKay of Lesley University's Sherrill Library; Kai Krause, who allowed us to use his "size of Africa" map; Dr. Karanja Carroll, Professor of Black Studies at Baruch College, for fact-checking; Professor Gérard Chouin of the College of William and Mary; my assistant, Esperanza Pacheco; and the countless cheerleaders who helped when my energy (and patience with the project) was flagging. I am additionally grateful to illustrator Hillary D. Wilson, designer Sara Yonas, and art director Laura Williams. The book is stunning because of all of you.

SOURCE NOTES

Introduction

The story of the hunter: Roger D. Abrahams, *African Folktales* (New York: Pantheon Books, 1983), 1.

Relative size of Africa: Sophie Morlin-Yron, "Why Do Western Maps Shrink Africa?" CNN, March 23, 2017, https://www.cnn.com/2016/08/18/africa/real-size-of-africa/index.html.

World languages: "World's Languages Traced Back to Single African Mother Tongue: Scientists." The World from PRX. Accessed November 14, 2018, https://www.pri.org/stories/2011-04-15/worlds-languages-traced-back-single-african-mother-tongue-scientists.

Kush, Nubia, and Meroë: National Geographic Society, Caryl-Sue. "The Kingdoms of Kush." National Geographic Society, July 2, 2018, https://www.nationalgeographic.org/media/kingdoms-kush/.

The Sahara Yawns

Ancient tools: Thomas Wynn, "Handaxe Enigmas," *World Archaeology* 27, no. 1 (1995): 10–24.

Brian Ludwig, "New Evidence for the Possible Use of Controlled Fire from ESA Sites in the Olduvai and Turkana Basins," *Abstracts for the Paleoanthropology Society Meeting,* The University of Pennsylvania Museum.

K. D. Schick and N. Toth, *Making Silent Stones Speak* (New York: Simon and Schuster, 1993), 160.

L. Wadley, T. Hodgskiss, and M. Grant, "From the Cover: Implications for complex cognition from the hafting tools with compound adhesives in the Middle Stone Age, South Africa." *Proceedings of the National Academy of Sciences of the United States of America* 106, no. 24 (June 2009); 9590–4, doi: 10.1073/pnas.0900957106.

Clapperton Chakanetsa Mavhunga, *Transient Workspaces* (Cambridge, MA: MIT Press, 2014), 17.

Ostrich waterspouts: Joseph Cornet, *A Survey of Zairian Art: the Bronson Collection* (Raleigh, NC: North Carolina Museum of Art, 1978), 155.

Changes to the Sahara: Lorraine Boissoneault, "What Really Turned the Sahara Desert From a Green Oasis Into a Wasteland?" Smithsonian.com, Smithsonian Institution, March 24, 2017, https://www.smithsonianmag.com/science-nature/what-really-turned-sahara-desert-green-oasis-wasteland-180962668/.

Menes: Creator of Dynasties

Unification of Upper and Lower Egypt: Noah Tesch, "Menes," Encyclopædia Britannica, Encyclopædia Britannica, inc., June 10, 2019, https://www.britannica.com/biography/Menes.

Burial traditions: Kara Cooney, *When Women Ruled the World: Six Queens of Egypt* (Washington, DC: National Geographic, 2020), 35–43.

Religion: Matt Stefon and Ugo Bianchi. "Dualism," Encyclopædia Britannica, Encyclopædia Britannica, inc., April 27, 2016, https://www.britannica.com/topic/dualism-religion.

Merneith: A Queen Erased

Royal life: Cooney, *When Women Ruled the World: Six Queens of Egypt*, 30–34.

Merneith stela: Joyce A. Tyldesley, *Chronicle of the Queens of Egypt: from Early Dynastic Times to the Death of Cleopatra*, (London: Thames & Hudson, 2006), 33.

Imhotep: From Peasant to God

Khasekhemwy and Nebka: "Khasekhemwy," Encyclopædia Britannica, Encyclopædia Britannica, inc., https://www.britannica.com/biography/Khasekhemwy.

Architecture: Jaromir Malek, "The Old Kingdom," *The Oxford History of Ancient Egypt* by Ian Shaw (ed.) (Oxford University Press, 2002), 92–93.

Egyptian medicine: UoMNews, "Egyptians, Not Greeks Were True Fathers of Medicine," EurekAlert!, May 9, 2007, https://www.eurekalert.org/pub_releases/2007-05/uom-eng050907.php.
Edwin Smith Surgical Papyrus: Gutenberg, Project. "Edwin Smith Surgical Papyrus." Edwin Smith Surgical Papyrus | Project Gutenberg Self-Publishing - eBooks | Read eBooks online. Accessed August 2, 2018. http://self.gutenberg.org/articles/edwin_smith_surgical_papyrus.

Quote by Sir William Osler: Noah Tesch, "Imhotep," Encyclopædia Britannica, inc., February 17, 2016, https://www.britannica.com/biography/Imhotep.

Transition to god: Dietrich, Wildung, *Egyptian Saints: Deification in Pharaonic Egypt* (New York: New York University Press, 1977), 34.
David Élisabeth, "Imhotep the Wise Deified," Louvre Museum (Paris, 2000), https://www.louvre.fr/en/oeuvre-notices/imhotep-wise-deified.

Inscription on Djoser's statue: Don Jaide, "Imhotep and Medical Science—Africa's Gift to the World," Rasta Livewire, June 8, 2007, https://www.africaresource.com/rasta/sesostris-the-great-the-egyptian-hercules/medical-science-africas-gift-to-the-world/.

Metal Bonds

Ancient metal working: H. Friede and R. Steel, "Iron Age Iron Smelting Furnaces of the Western/Central Transvaal: Their Structure, Typology and Affinities," *The South African Archaeological Bulletin* 40, no. 141 (1985): 45, https://doi.org/10.2307/3887993. *Metals in Past Societies*, 17–30, 33–56, 61–88, 108–120, 136–141.

Smelting techniques: Thorsten Severin, Thilo Rehren, and Helmut Schleicher, "Early Metal Smelting in Aksum, Ethiopia: Copper or Iron?" *European Journal of Mineralogy* 23, no. 6 (2011): 981–92, https://doi.org/10.1127/0935-1221/2011/0023-2167.

Nature as Character

"Tale of an Old Woman": Abrahams, *African Folktales*, 57–58.

"The King's Daughter Who Lost Her Hair": Abrahams, *African Folktales*, 59–63.

Aesop: The Wisest Man in the Ancient World

Fables and history: Aesopus and Lloyd W. Daly, *Aesop without Morals: the Famous Fables and a Life of Aesop* (New York: Yoseloff, 1963), 89–90.

Biography: "Aesop," Encyclopedia.com, October 8, 2020, https://www.encyclopedia.com/people/literature-and-arts/classical-literature-biographies/aesop.

The Girl and the Rose Red Slippers: Aesop. "The Girl with the Rose Red Slippers," Ancient Egypt: the Mythology—The Girl with the Rose Red Slippers. Accessed January 15, 2018. http://www.egyptianmyths.net/mythslippers.htm.

The Eagle and the Beetle: Aesop (adapted). "Aesop's Fables," Aesop's Fables—Timeless Stories with a Moral. Accessed October 16, 2020. https://aesopsfables.org/.

Across the Waves

Ancient Carthage: Patrick Hunt. "Carthage," Encyclopædia Britannica, Encyclopædia Britannica, inc., July 14, 2020, https://www.britannica.com/place/Carthage-ancient-city-Tunisia.

Hannibal Barca: Unparalleled Military Strategist

Biography: The Editors of Encyclopaedia Britannica, "Hannibal," Encyclopædia Britannica, Encyclopædia Britannica, inc. Accessed April 21, 2019, https://www.britannica.com/biography/Hannibal-Carthaginian-general-247-183-BC.

Hamilcar Barca: The Editors of Encyclopaedia Britannica, "Hamilcar Barca," Encyclopædia Britannica, Encyclopædia Britannica, inc. Accessed April 21, 2019, https://www.britannica.com/biography/Hamilcar-Barca.

Punic Wars: Michael Ray, "Punic Wars," Encyclopædia Britannica, Encyclopædia Britannica, inc., July 10, 2017, https://www.britannica.com/event/Punic-Wars.

Terence: North African Playwright

Biography: "Terence—Terence Biography—Poem Hunter," PoemHunter.com. Accessed May 13, 2020. https://www.poemhunter.com/terence/biography/.
W. Geoffrey Arnott, "Terence," Encyclopædia Britannica, Encyclopædia Britannica, inc., July 20, 1998, https://www.britannica.com/biography/Terence.

Plays: Alice B. Fort and Herbert S. Kates, "Publius Terentius Afer ('Terence')," Grosset & Dunlap. Accessed June 2, 2019, http://theatrehistory.com/ancient/terence007.html.

Amanirenas: Warrior, Diplomat, Queen

Biography: Mariam F. Ayad, "The Pyramid Texts Of Amenirdis I: Selection And Layout," *Journal of the American Research Center in Egypt* 43 (2007): 71–92. Accessed August 12, 2019, http://www.jstor.org/stable/27801607.
Jason Porath, "Amanirenas: The One-Eyed Queen Who Fought Rome Tooth and Nail," Rejected Princesses. Accessed August 12, 2019. https://www.rejectedprincesses.com/princesses/amanirenas.
"Statue of Queen and Prince of Meroë," Museums for Intercultural Dialogue. Accessed August 12, 2019, http://www.unesco.org/culture/museum-for-dialogue/item/en/84/statue-of-queen-and-prince-of-meroe.
Clyde Winters, "Prince Akinidad of Kush and the One Eyed Kandake in the Meroite-Roman War," Ancient Origins, October 21, 2016, https://www.ancient-origins.net/history-famous-people/prince-akinidad-kush-and-one-eyed-kandake-meroite-roman-war-006854.

Where Few Dared to Tread

Beginnings of trans-Saharan trade: "World Eras. Encyclopedia.com. 30 Sep. 2020." Encyclopedia.com. Encyclopedia.com, October 15, 2020, https://www.encyclopedia.com/history/news-wires-white-papers-and-books/trans-saharan-caravan-trade.

Tin Hinan: Founding a City on the Dunes

Biography: "Queen Tin Hinan: Founder of the Tuaregs," Think Africa, July 14, 2019, https://thinkafrica.net/tin-hinan/.

Tuareg people: "The Ancient Tuaregs, Lost Lords of the Sahara," Ancient Origins, April 13, 2015, https://www.ancient-origins.net/history/ancient-tuaregs-lost-lords-sahara-002900.

"The Tuareg Clans: a Complete Matriarchy and Men in Burkas," Mysteries24.com. Accessed October 15, 2020. https://mysteries24. com/n3-82353-The_Tuareg_Clans:_a_Complete_Matriarchy_and_Men_ in_Burkas.

Tomb: "The Monumental Tomb of Queen Tin Hinan, Ancient Ancestress of the Tuaregs," Ancient Origins, January 17, 2020, https://www. ancient-origins.net/history-famous-people/monumental-tomb-queen-tin-hinan-ancient-ancestress-tuaregs-002833.

Across the Golden Sand

Sahara desert: Jeffrey Allman Gritzner and Ronald Francis Peel, "Study and Exploration," Encyclopædia Britannica, inc., November 26, 2019, https://www.britannica.com/place/Sahara-desert-Africa/ Study-and-exploration.

Salt Mines: https://www.ancient.eu/article/1342/ the-salt-trade-of-ancient-west-africa/.

Kathleen Bickford Berzock, Ronald A. Messier, and Abdullah Fili, "Sijilmasa's Role in the African Gold Trade," *Caravans of Gold, Fragments in Time: Art, Culture, and Exchange across Medieval Saharan Africa* (Evanston, IL: Block Museum of Art, Northwestern University, 2019), 115.

Nehemia Levtzion and John F. P. Hopkins, eds, Corpus of Early Arabic Sources for West Africa (New York: Marcus Weiner Press, 2000), 76, 399.

Gold trade: Kathleen Bickford Berzock and Ralph A. Austen, "The Sources of Gold," *Caravans of Gold, Fragments in Time: Art, Culture, and Exchange across Medieval Saharan Africa* (Evanston, IL: Block Museum of Art, Northwestern University, 2019), 63–68.

"The Trans-Saharan Gold Trade (7th–14th Century)," Department of the Arts of Africa, Oceania, and the Americas, The Metropolitan Museum of Art, October 2000, https://www.metmuseum.org/toah/ hd/gold/hd_gold.htm.

Image: Warren M. Robbins and Nancy Ingram Nooter, *African Art in American Collections*.

Mansa Musa: The Richest Man of All Time

Biography: Henry Louis Gates, *100 Amazing Facts About the Negro* (New York: Random House Inc, 2017), 182–183.

N. Levtzion, "The Thirteenth- and Fourteenth-Century Kings of Mali," *The Journal of African History* 4, no. 3 (1963), 341–353.

Linda McDowell and Marilyn Mackay, 2005. *Teacher's Guide for World History Societies of the Past* (Winnipeg, Canada: Portage and Main Press, 2005), 246.

John Thornton, *Africa and Africans in the Making of the Atlantic World: 1400–1800* (Cambridge, UK: Cambridge University Press, 2007), 16–18.

Abubakari II: Joan Baxter, "AFRICA: Africa's 'Greatest Explorer,'" BBC News, BBC, December 13, 2000, http://news.bbc.co.uk/2/hi/africa/1068950. stm.

Basil Davidson, *The Lost Cities of Africa* (Boston: Little, Brown and Company, 2007), 74–75.

Ivan Van Sertima, *African Presence in Early America* (New Brunswick, NJ: Transaction Publishers, 2000), 35–36, 66.

Ivan Van Sertima, *They Came before Columbus: the African Presence in Ancient America* (New York: Random House Trade Paperbacks, 2003), 27–28, 39–50.

Mali empire: Kathleen Bickford Berzock and Robert Launay, "Views from Afar," *Caravans of Gold, Fragments in Time: Art, Culture, and Exchange across Medieval Saharan Africa* (Evanston, IL: Block Museum of Art, Northwestern University, 2019), 54, 178.

David C. Conrad, *Great Empires of the Past: Empires of Medieval West Africa: Ghana, Mali, and Songhay* (New York: Facts on File, Inc., 2009), 45.

Cheikh Anta Diop and Harold J. Salemson, Essay, *Precolonial Black Africa: a Comparative Study of the Political and Social Systems of Europe and Black Africa, from Antiquity to the Formation of Modern States* (Chicago: Chicago Review Press, 2012), 101–113.

"The Empire of Mali (1230–1600)," South African History Online. Accessed June 8, 2018. https://www.sahistory.org.za/article/empire-mali-1230-1600.

Saharan routes: Kathleen Bickford Berzock, "Caravans of Gold, Fragments in Time: An Introduction," *Caravans of Gold, Fragments in Time: Art, Culture, and Exchange across Medieval Saharan Africa* (Evanston, IL: Block Museum of Art, Northwestern University, 2019), 25.

Gold: Kathleen Bickford Berzock and Sarah M. Guérin, "Gold, Ivory, and Copper," *Caravans of Gold, Fragments in Time: Art, Culture, and Exchange across Medieval Saharan Africa* (Evanston, IL: Block Museum of Art, Northwestern University, 2019), 178.

The Catalan Atlas

Catalan Atlas: Berzock, "Caravans of Gold, Fragments in Time: An Introduction," *Caravans of Gold, Fragments in Time: Art, Culture, and Exchange across Medieval Saharan Africa*, 23–25.

The Power of the Griot

Otsman's response to Musa: Msw, "The Armies of Ghana and Songhai," Weapons and Warfare, May 9, 2016, https://weaponsandwarfare.com/2016/05/11/the-armies-of-ghana-and-songhai/.

Libraries in the Sand

Timbuktu: Diop and Salemson, Essay, *Precolonial Black Africa: a Comparative Study of the Political and Social Systems of Europe and Black Africa, from Antiquity to the Formation of Modern States*, 113–74.

Hidden manuscripts: BBC, "0:40 / 59:31 BBC: The Lost Libraries of Timbuktu," YouTube, British Broadcasting Corporation, September 2, 2015, https://www.youtube.com/watch?reload=9.

Joshua Hammer, *The Bad-Ass Librarians of Timbuktu and Their Race to Save the World's Most Precious Manuscripts* (New York: Simon & Schuster, 2016), 3–29.

The Winds of Change

Changes in ships and sailing methods: Thornton, *Africa and Africans in the Making of the Atlantic World: 1400–1800*, 23–56.

Gérard Chouin, Associate Professor of History from the College of William & Mary, Email, June 4, 2020.

Queen Idia of Esigie

Igala people: The Editors of Encyclopaedia Britannica, "Igala," Encyclopædia Britannica, inc., August 22, 2019, https://www.britannica.com/topic/Igala.

Biography: Alexander Ives Bortolot, "Women Leaders in African History: Idia, First Queen Mother of Benin," metmuseum.org, October 2003, https://www.metmuseum.org/toah/hd/pwmn_3/hd_pwmn_3.htm.

Queen Idia's pendant: "Queen Mother Pendant Mask: Iyoba 16th Century," Arts of Africa, Oceania, and the Americas, metmuseum.org. Accessed October 8, 2020. https://www.metmuseum.org/toah/works-of-art/1978.412.323/.

Yael Biro, Associate Curator, Department of Africa, Oceania, and the Americas, Interview November 1, 2018.

Benin bronzes: "Benin Plaques at the British Museum (Article)," Khan Academy. Accessed November 3, 2018. https://www.khanacademy.org/humanities/art-africa/west-africa/nigeria/a/benin-plaques. Biro, Interview.

Culture Lost

European interest in colonizing Africa: Saul David, PhD, "History—British History in Depth: Slavery and the 'Scramble for Africa,'" BBC, February 17, 2011, http://www.bbc.co.uk/history/british/abolition/scramble_for_africa_article_01.shtml.

Destruction of manuscripts: BBC, "0:40 / 59:31 BBC: The Lost Libraries of Timbuktu," YouTube, British Broadcasting Corporation, September 2, 2015, https://www.youtube.com/watch?reload=9.

Emperor Tewodoros II: The Editors of Encyclopaedia Britannica, "Tewodros II," Encyclopædia Britannica, inc., 1998, https://www.britannica.com/biography/Tewodros-II.

Yoruba math: Claudia Zaslavsky, "Mathematics of the Yoruba People and of Their Neighbors in Southern Nigeria," *The Two-Year College Mathematics Journal* 1, no. 2 (1970): 76. https://doi.org/10.2307/3027363.

African Stonehenge: Eric Betz, "Nabta Playa: The World's First Astronomical Site Was Built in Africa," Astronomy.com, June 20, 2020, https://astronomy.com/news/2020/06/nabta-playa-the-worlds-first-astronomical-site-was-built-in-africa-and-is-older-than-stonehenge.

Recent archaeological discoveries: Owen Jarus, "The 10 Biggest Archaeology Discoveries of 2019," LiveScience, Purch, December 26, 2019. https://www.livescience.com/biggest-archaeology-discoveries-2019.html.

Venetian glass beads in Lake Chad art: Biro, Interview.

Author's Note

Wealth in Africa: Nick, Dearden, "Africa Is Not Poor, We Are Stealing Its Wealth," Africa, Al Jazeera, May 24, 2017, https://www.aljazeera.com/indepth/opinion/2017/05/africa-poor-stealing-wealth-170524063731884.html.

Photo Credits

Page 99 (turtle), Wikimedia Commons; pages 112–113 (Catalan Atlas), Wikimedia Commons; page 81 (kandake stela), Wikimedia Commons; page 132 (Idia mask), Metropolitan Museum of Art / Open Access

BIBLIOGRAPHY

Abrahams, Roger D. *African Folktales*. New York: Pantheon Books, 1983.

Aesop. "Aesop's Fables." Aesop's Fables—Timeless Stories with a Moral. Accessed October 16, 2020. https://aesopsfables.org/.

Aesop. "The Girl with the Rose Red Slippers." Ancient Egypt: the Mythology— The Girl with the Rose Red Slippers. Accessed January 15, 2018. http:// www.egyptianmyths.net/mythslippers.htm.

"Aesop." Encyclopedia.com, October 8, 2020. https://www.encyclopedia.com/ people/literature-and-arts/classical-literature-biographies/aesop.

Aesopus and Lloyd W. Daly. *Aesop without Morals: the Famous Fables and a Life of Aesop*. New York: Yoseloff, 1963.

Arnott, W. Geoffrey. "Terence." Encyclopædia Britannica, inc., July 20, 1998. https://www.britannica.com/biography/Terence.

"Queen Mother Pendant Mask: Iyoba 16th Century." Arts of Africa, Oceania, and the Americas. metmuseum.org. Accessed October 8, 2020. https://www.metmuseum.org/toah/works-of-art/1978.412.323/.

Ayad, Mariam F. "The Pyramid Texts of Amenirdis I: Selection and Layout." *Journal of the American Research Center in Egypt*, 2007, 71–92.

Barton, Marc. "Imhotep—The First Physician." Medical Exam Prep, July 18, 2018. https://www.medicalexamprep.co.uk/imhotep-first-physician/.

Baxter, Joan. "AFRICA: Africa's 'Greatest Explorer.'" BBC News. BBC, December 13, 2000. http://news.bbc.co.uk/2/hi/africa/1068950.stm.

Berzock, Kathleen Bickford. *Caravans of Gold, Fragments in Time Art, Culture, and Exchange across Medieval Saharan Africa*. Evanston, IL: Block Museum of Art, Northwestern University, 2019.

Betz, Eric. "Nabta Playa: The World's First Astronomical Site Was Built in Africa." Astronomy.com, June 20, 2020. https://astronomy.com/ news/2020/06/nabta-playa-the-worlds-first-astronomical-site-was-built-in-africa-and-is-older-than-stonehenge.

Biersteker, Ann. "Kujibizana: Questions of Language and Power in Nineteenth- and Twentieth-Century Poetry in Kishwahili." Project MUSE. Michigan State University Press, 1996. https://muse.jhu.edu/ chapter/821592/pdf.

Boissoneault, Lorraine. "What Really Turned the Sahara Desert From a Green Oasis Into a Wasteland?" Smithsonian.com. Smithsonian Institution, March 24, 2017. https://www.smithsonianmag.com/ science-nature/what-really-turned-sahara-desert-green-oasis-wasteland-180962668/.

Bortolot, Alexander Ives. "Women Leaders in African History: Idia, First Queen Mother of Benin." metmuseum.org, October 2003. https:// www.metmuseum.org/toah/hd/pwmn_3/hd_pwmn_3.htm.

Caesar, Julius, James Hamilton, and Thomas Clark. *Caesar's Commentaries.* Chicago: Farquhar & Albright Co., 1884.

Chirikure, Shadreck. *Metals in Past Societies: A Global Perspective on Indigenous African Metallurgy.* New York: Springer, 2015.

Conrad, David C. *Empires of Medieval West Africa: Ghana, Mali, and Songhay.* New York: Chelsea House Publishers, 2010.

Cooney, Kara. *When Women Ruled the World: Six Queens of Egypt.* Washington, D.C.: National Geographic, 2020.

Cornet, Joseph. *A Survey of Zairian Art: the Bronson Collection.* Raleigh, NC: North Carolina Museum of Art, 1978.

David, Saul, PhD. "History—British History in Depth: Slavery and the 'Scramble for Africa.'" BBC, February 17, 2011. http://www.bbc.co.uk/history/british/abolition/scramble_for_africa_article_01.shtml.

Davidson, Basil. *The Lost Cities of Africa.* Boston: Little, Brown and Company, 2007.

Dearden, Nick. "Africa Is Not Poor, We Are Stealing Its Wealth." Africa, Al Jazeera, May 24, 2017. https://www.aljazeera.com/indepth/opinion/2017/05/africa-poor-stealing-wealth-170524063731884.html.

"The Trans-Saharan Gold Trade (7th–14th Century)." Department of the Arts of Africa, Oceania, and the Americas. The Metropolitan Museum of Art, October 2000. https://www.metmuseum.org/toah/hd/gold/hd_gold.htm.

Diop, Cheikh Anta, and Harold J. Salemson. *Precolonial Black Africa: a Comparative Study of the Political and Social Systems of Europe and Black Africa, from Antiquity to the Formation of Modern States* (Chicago: Chicago Review Press, 2012), 113–74.

The Editors of Encyclopaedia Britannica. "Hannibal." Encyclopædia Britannica. Encyclopædia Britannica, inc. Accessed April 21, 2019. https://www.britannica.com/biography/Hannibal-Carthaginian-general-247-183-BC.

The Editors of Encyclopaedia Britannica. "Igala." Encyclopædia Britannica. Encyclopædia Britannica, inc., August 22, 2019. https://www.britannica.com/topic/Igala.

The Editors of Encyclopaedia Britannica. "Imhotep." Encyclopædia Britannica. Encyclopædia Britannica, inc., November 11, 2019. https://www.britannica.com/biography/Imhotep.

The Editors of Encyclopaedia Britannica. "Kashta." Encyclopædia Britannica. Encyclopædia Britannica, inc., November 5, 2019. https://www.britannica.com/biography/Kashta.

The Editors of Encyclopaedia Britannica. "Tewodros II." Encyclopædia Britannica. Encyclopædia Britannica, inc., 1998. https://www.britannica.com/biography/Tewodros-II.

"The Empire of Mali (1230-1600)." South African History Online. Accessed October 8, 2020. https://www.sahistory.org.za/article/empire-mali-1230-1600.

Friede, H., and R. Steel. "Iron Age Iron Smelting Furnaces of the Western/ Central Transvaal: Their Structure, Typology and Affinities." *The South African Archaeological Bulletin* 40, no. 141 (1985): 45. https://doi. org/10.2307/3887993.

Gates, Henry Louis. *100 Amazing Facts About the Negro.* New York: Random House Inc, 2017.

Griffiths, Sarah. "King Aha: First Pharaoh Ruled Ancient Egypt 500 Years LATER than First Thought." Daily Mail Online. Associated Newspapers, September 3, 2013. https://www.dailymail.co.uk/ sciencetech/article-2410047/King-Aha-First-pharaoh-ruled-Ancient-Egypt-500-years-LATER-thought.html.

Gritzner, Jeffrey Allman, and Ronald Francis Peel. "Study and Exploration." Encyclopædia Britannica. Encyclopædia Britannica, inc., November 26, 2019. https://www.britannica.com/place/Sahara-desert-Africa/ Study-and-exploration.

Gutenberg, Project. "Edwin Smith Surgical Papyrus." Edwin Smith Surgical Papyrus | Project Gutenberg Self-Publishing - eBooks | Read eBooks online. Accessed August 2, 2018. http://self.gutenberg.org/articles/ edwin_smith_surgical_papyrus.

Hammer, Joshua. *The Bad-Ass Librarians of Timbuktu: And Their Race to Save the Worlds Most Precious Manuscripts.* New York: Simon & Schuster, 2016.

"History—Imhotep." BBC. Accessed October 8, 2020. http://www.bbc.co.uk/ history/historic_figures/imhotep.shtml.

"History of Ethiopia According to Herodotus,Diodorus & Strabo Research." Scribd. Accessed October 8, 2020. https://www.scribd.com/ document/37307363/History-of-Ethiopia-According-to-Herodotus-Diodorus-Strabo-Research.

Hunt, Patrick. "Carthage." Encyclopædia Britannica. Encyclopædia Britannica, inc., July 14, 2020. https://www.britannica.com/place/ Carthage-ancient-city-Tunisia.

Jaide, Don. "Imhotep and Medical Science—Africa's Gift to the World." Rasta Livewire, June 8, 2007. https://www.africaresource. com/rasta/sesostris-the-great-the-egyptian-hercules/ medical-science-africas-gift-to-the-world/.

Jarus, Owen. "The 10 Biggest Archaeology Discoveries of 2019." LiveScience. Purch, December 26, 2019. https://www.livescience.com/biggest-archaeology-discoveries-2019.html.

"King Piankhi." Encyclopedia.com, October 8, 2020. https://www.encyclopedia.com/history/ encyclopedias-almanacs-transcripts-and-maps/king-piankhi.

"Kingdom of Ghana." Ancient Civilizations, n.d. Kingdom of Ghana.

Levtzion, N. "The Thirteenth- and Fourteenth-Century Kings of Mali." *The Journal of African History* 4, no. 3 (1963): 341–53. https://doi.org/10.1017/ s002185370000428x.

Ludwig, Brian. "New Evidence for the Possible Use of Controlled Fire from ESA Sites in the Olduvai and Turkana Basins." *Abstracts for the Paleoanthropology Society Meeting, The University of Pennsylvania Museum*, n.d.

"Mansa Abubakari II." Encyclopedia.com, October 8, 2020. https://www.encyclopedia.com/history/news-wires-white-papers-and-books/mansa-abubakari-ii.

Mavhunga, Clapperton Chakanetsa. *Transient Workspaces: Technologies of Everyday Innovation in Zimbabwe*. Cambridge, MA: MIT Press, 2014.

McDowell, Linda, and Marilyn Mackay. *Teacher's Guide for World History Societies of the Past*. Winnipeg, Canada: Portage & Main Press, 2005.

Morlin-Yron, Sophie. "Why Do Western Maps Shrink Africa?" CNN. Cable News Network, March 23, 2017. https://www.cnn.com/2016/08/18/africa/real-size-of-africa/index.html.

Msw. "The Armies of Ghana and Songhai." Weapons and Warfare, May 9, 2016. https://weaponsandwarfare.com/2016/05/11/the-armies-of-ghana-and-songhai/.

National Geographic Society, Caryl-Sue. "The Kingdoms of Kush." National Geographic Society, July 2, 2018. https://www.nationalgeographic.org/media/kingdoms-kush/.

"Nubia Gallery." Kushite Kingdom, The Oriental Institute of the University of Chicago. Accessed October 8, 2020. https://oi.uchicago.edu/museum-exhibits/nubia/kushite-kingdom.

"Plant Bedding, Medicinal Plant Use, and Settlement Patterns at Sibidu." *University of the Witwatersrand*, December 2011.

Porath, Jason. "Amanirenas: The One-Eyed Queen Who Fought Rome Tooth and Nail." Rejected Princesses. Accessed October 8, 2020. https://www.rejectedprincesses.com/princesses/amanirenas.

Ray, Michael. "Punic Wars." Encyclopædia Britannica. Encyclopædia Britannica, inc., July 10, 2017. https://www.britannica.com/event/Punic-Wars.

Robbins, Warren M., and Nancy Ingram. Nooter. *African Art in American Collections: Survey 1989*. Atglen, PA: Schiffer Pub., 2004.

Schick, Kathy Diane, and Nicholas Toth. *Making Silent Stones Speak: Human Evolution and the Dawn of Technology*. London: Phoenix, 1995.

Sertima, Ivan Van. *African Presence in Early America*. New Brunswick, NJ: Transaction Publishers, 2000.

Sertima, Ivan Van. *They Came before Columbus: the African Presence in Ancient America*. New York: Random House Trade Paperbacks, 2003.

Severin, Thorsten, Thilo Rehren, and Helmut Schleicher. "Early Metal Smelting in Aksum, Ethiopia: Copper or Iron?" *European Journal of Mineralogy* 23, no. 6 (2011): 981–92. https://doi.org/10.1127/0935-1221/2011/0023-2167.

"Statue of Queen and Prince of Meroë." Museums for Intercultural Dialogue—Statue of queen and prince of Meroë. Accessed October 8,

2020. http://www.unesco.org/culture/museum-for-dialogue/item/en/84/statue-of-queen-and-prince-of-meroe.

Stefon, Matt, and Ugo Bianchi. "Dualism." Encyclopædia Britannica. Encyclopædia Britannica, inc., April 27, 2016. https://www.britannica.com/topic/dualism-religion.

"Terence—Terence Biography—Poem Hunter." PoemHunter.com. Accessed May 13, 2020. https://www.poemhunter.com/terence/biography/.

Tesch, Noah. "Menes." Encyclopædia Britannica. Encyclopædia Britannica, inc., June 10, 2019. https://www.britannica.com/biography/Menes.

Thomas, Wynn. "Handaxe Enigmas." *World Archaeology* 27, no. 1 (1995): 10–24.

Thornton, John. *Africa and Africans in the Making of the Atlantic World: 1400–1800*. Cambridge, UK: Cambridge University Press, 2007.

"The Trans-Saharan Caravan Trade." Encyclopedia.com, October 8, 2020. https://www.encyclopedia.com/history/news-wires-white-papers-and-books/trans-saharan-caravan-trade.

Trimingham, John Spencer. *A History of Islam in West Africa*. Oxford, UK: Oxford University Press, 1985.

Tyldesley, Joyce A. *Chronicle of the Queens of Egypt: from Early Dynastic Times to the Death of Cleopatra*. London: Thames & Hudson, 2006.

UoMNews. "Egyptians, Not Greeks Were True Fathers of Medicine." EurekAlert!, May 9, 2007. https://www.eurekalert.org/pub_releases/2007-05/uom-eng050907.php.

"The 'Voyager King' Mansa Abubakari II—Africa's Greatest Explorer." Muslim News Magazine. Accessed October 8, 2020. http://www.muslimnewsmagazine.tv/abubakari.html.

Wadley, L., T. Hodgskiss, and M. Grant. "Implications for Complex Cognition from the Hafting of Tools with Compound Adhesives in the Middle Stone Age, South Africa." *Proceedings of the National Academy of Sciences* 106, no. 24 (2009): 9590–94. https://doi.org/10.1073/pnas.0900957106.

Wildung, Dietrich. *Egyptian Saints: Deification in Pharaonic Egypt*. New York: New York University Press, 1977.

Winters, Clyde. "Prince Akinidad of Kush and the One Eyed Kandake in the Meroite-Roman War." Ancient Origins, October 21, 2016. https://www.ancient-origins.net/history-famous-people/prince-akinidad-kush-and-one-eyed-kandake-meroite-roman-war-006854.

"World's Languages Traced Back to Single African Mother Tongue: Scientists." The World from PRX. GlobalNews, April 15, 2011. https://www.pri.org/stories/2011-04-15/worlds-languages-traced-back-single-african-mother-tongue-scientists.

Zaslavsky, Claudia. "Mathematics of the Yoruba People and of Their Neighbors in Southern Nigeria." *The Two-Year College Mathematics Journal* 1, no. 2 (1970): 76. https://doi.org/10.2307/3027363.

FURTHER EXPLORATION

Africa's Great Civilizations, PBS, www.pbs.org/weta/africas-great-civilizations/home/.

Exploring Africa, African Studies Center, Michigan State University, http://exploringafrica.matrix.msu.edu/.

"The Powerful Stories that Shaped Africa," Gus Casely-Hayford, TEDGlobal 2017, www.ted.com/talks/gus_casely_hayford_the_powerful_stories_that_shaped_africa.

"What's the Real Size of Africa?" CNN, www.cnn.com/2016/08/18/africa/real-size-of-africa/index.html.

The Lost Libraries of Timbuktu, https://www.youtube.com/watch?reload=9&v=BzBCl9kcdqc.

INDEX

DESIGNER'S NOTE

When I was asked to design this book, I felt thrilled and privileged to be chosen to accompany Tracey Baptiste's words and Hillary D. Wilson's images with an afrocentric design concept. Immediately I thought about the design in a variety of ways, and what became a recurring thought was to make this book a visual statement for Africa and the young readers in its diaspora. *African Icons* had to not only speak to our design tradition with a rich visual vernacular, but it also had to point to the future, to inspire emerging creatives to bask in our glorious design history.

Every icon profiled in this book represents specific times and places in history that are often referenced only in words. I wanted to find a way to contextualize them authentically, so I framed each chapter with a graphic pattern borrowed from ancient African tradition and repurposed in modern digital fashion. It was important to show that it is possible to adapt ancestral African traditions to the present in a dignified and faithful manner, without stripping them of their original symbolism or historical significance. I hope the visual elements of *African Icons* will enrich the stories of these individuals and inspire readers to learn more about the rich history of Africa.